March of America Facsimile Series

Number 5

Divers Voyages

Richard Hakluyt

Divers Voyages Touching the Discoverie of America

by Richard Hakluyt

ANN ARBOR

UNIVERSITY MICROFILMS, INC.

A Subsidiary of Xerox Corporation

Foreword

Divers voyages touching the discouerie of America was printed in London in 1582 with no indication of authorship other than the initials R. H. at the end of the dedication, but the author is known to have been Richard Hakluyt the younger, who later compiled the great collection of voyage literature entitled *The Principall nauigations, voiages and discoueries of the English nation.* Hakluyt's interest in geography and exploration had first been kindled by his older cousin of the same name, a lawyer of the Middle Temple, who was tireless in his own efforts to encourage English colonization of the New World.

Hakluyt's dedication declared his conviction that the time had come for Englishmen to follow the example of the Spanish and Portuguese in taking a share of the new lands, where the idle surplus population of England could be settled. The narratives included in the volume were designed to provide his countrymen with what was known of North America from the Cabot voyages (which he stressed as the basis of English claims), the mythical voyage of the Zeno brothers, Verrazano's exploration and that of Jacques Cartier, and an account of Jean Ribaut's colony in Florida. Hakluyt added the "Booke of Robert Thorne," two lettters exhorting Henry VIII to explore the northern parts of America, because of Thorne's clear statement of an expansionist policy that Hakluyt himself favored. He prefaced his book with a note on the probability of a Northwest Passage and appended two notes prepared by his cousin as instructions for potential colonizers and a list of valuable commodities to be looked for in America. The compilation was thus planned as a manual that would give would-be colonists facts about the lands as yet unclaimed by other nations. It was also designed to encourage them to undertake new ventures by appealing to their love of country and desire for glory and profit and their zeal as Christians to convert heathen peoples. To the younger Hakluyt, a preacher himself, the last motive had the greatest force; in his dedication he expressed the opinion that recent efforts had failed because they were animated more by love of gain than by zeal "for the aduauncement of the kingdome of Christ, and the enlargement of his glorious Gospell."

The publication of *Divers voyages* brought Hakluyt to the attention of Sir Francis Walsingham, Queen Elizabeth's Secretary of State, who commended Hakluyt's efforts and gave him a mission to perform in connection with the projected colony by Sir Humphrey Gilbert. Until his death in 1616 Hakluyt continued to further English colonization with religious zeal by further writings, private persuasion, and active participation in the planning and formation of schemes for settlement of America.

Divers voyages has been reprinted by the Hakluyt Society with an introduction and notes by John Winter Jones (London, 1850). The activities of Hakluyt and his cousin are described in George B. Parks, *Richard Hakluyt and the English Voyages* (New York, 1928) and E. G. R. Taylor, ed., *The Writings and Correspondence of the Two Richard Hakluyts* (2 vols., London, 1935).

Divers Voyages

DIVERS

voyages touching the difcouerie of
America, *and the Ilands adiacent*
vnto the fame, made firft of all by our
*Englifhmen, and afterward by the French-
men and Britons:*

And certaine notes of aduertifements for obferua-
tions, neceffarie for fuch as fhall heereafter
make the like attempt,

With two mappes annexed heereunto for the
plainer vnderftanding of the whole
matter.

Imprinted at Lon-

don for Thomas VVoodcocke,
dwelling in paules Church-yard,
at the figne of the blacke beare.

1582.

❧ The names of certaine late writers of Geographie, with the yeere wherein they wrote.

The

The names of certaine late trauay-
lers, both by sea and by lande, which
also for the moſt part haue written of
their owne trauayles and voyages.

The yere of
our Lorde.

1178	Beniamin Tudelenſis a Iewe.
1270	Marcus Paulus a Venetian.
1300	Harton an Armenian.
1320	Iohn Mandeuile knight, engliſhman.
1380	Nicolaus and Antonius Zeni, venetians.
1444	Nicolaus Conti venetian.
1492	Chriſtopher Columbus a Genoway.
1497	Sebaſtian Gabot, an egnliſhman the ſonne of a venetiã.
1497	M. Thorne and Hugh Eleot of Briſtowe, engliſhmen.
1497	Vaſques de Gama a portingale.
1500	Gaſper Corterealis a portingale.
1516	Edoardus Barboſa a portingale.
1519	Fernandus Magalianes a portingale.
1530	Iohn Barros a portingale.
1534	Iaques Cartier a Briton.
1540	Francis Vaſques de Coronado Spaniarde.
1542	Iohn Gaetan Spaniarde.
1549	Francis Xauier a portingale.
1553	Hugh Willowbie knight, & Richard Chauncellor Eng.
1554	Francis Galuano a portingale.
1556	Stenen and William Burros Engliſhmen.
1562	Antonie Ienkinſon Engliſhman.
1562	Iohn Ribault a Frenchman.
1565	Andrewe Theuet a Frenchman.
1576	Martin Frobiſher Engliſhman.
1578	Francis Drake Engliſhman.
1580	Arthur Pet, and Charles Iackmã Engliſhmen.
1582	Edwarde Fenton, and Luke warde, Engliſhmen.
1582	Humfrey Gilbert knight, Edward Heyes, and Antonie Brigham Engliſhmen.

A verie late and great probabilitie of a passage, by the Northwest part of America in 58.degrees of Northerly latitude.

An excellent learned man of portingale, of singuler grauety, authoritie and experience tolde mee very lately, that one *Anus Cortereal*, captayne of the yle of Tercera about the yeere 1574. which is not aboue eight yeres past, sent a Shippe to discouer the Northwest passage of America, & that the same shippe arriuing on the coast of the saide America in fiftie eyghte degrees of latitude, founde a great entrance exceeding deepe and broade, without all impediment of ice, into whiche they passed aboue twentie leagues, and found it alwaies to trende towarde the South, the lande lying lowe and plaine on eyther side: And that they perswaded them selues verely, that there was a way open into the south sea. But their victailes fayling them, and being but one shippe, they returned backe agayne with ioy. This place seemeth to lie in equal degrees of latitude, with the first entrance of the sounde of Denmark betweene Norway and the head land, called in latin *Cimbrorum promontorium*, and therefore like to bee open and nauigable a great part of the yeere. And this report may bee well annexed vnto the other eight reasons mentioned in my epistle dedicatorie, for proofe of the likelihood of this passage by the Northwest.

❧ To the right worſhipfull and moſt vertuous Gentleman maſter Phillip Sydney Eſquire.

Maruaile not a little (right wor-ſhipfull) that ſince the firſt diſco-uerie of America (which is nowe full foureſcore and tenne yeeres) after ſo great conqueſts and plan-tings of the Spaniardes and Por-tingales there, that wee of Eng-lande could neuer haue the grace to ſet faſt footing in ſuch fer-till and temperate places, as are left as yet vnpoſſeſſed of them. But againe when I conſider that there is a time for all men, and ſee the Portingales time to be out of date, & that the nakedneſſe of the ſpaniards, and their long hidden ſecretes are nowe at length eſpied, whereby they went about to delude the worlde, I conceiue great hope, that the time approcheth and nowe is, that we of England may ſhare and part ſtakes (if wee will our ſelues) both with the ſpaniarde and the Portingale in part of America, and other regions as yet vndiſcouered. And ſurely if there were in vs that deſire to aduaunce the honour of our Countrie which ought to bee in euery good man, wee woulde not all this while haue fore-ſlowne the poſſeſſing of thoſe landes, whiche of equitie and right appertaine vnto vs, as by the diſcourſes that followe ſhall appeare moſt plainely. Yea if wee woulde beholde with the eye of pitie howe al our Priſons are peſtered and filled with able men to ſerue their Countrie, which for ſmall roberies are dayly hanged vp in great numbers euen twentie at a clappe out of one iayle (as was ſeene at the laſt aſſiſes at Rocheſter) wee woulde haſten and further euery man to his power the deduc-ting of ſome Colonies of our ſuperfluous people into thoſe tem-perate and fertile partes of America, which being within ſixe

weekes

The Epiftle

weekes fayling of England are yet vnpoffeffed by any Chriftians:
and feeme to offer themfelues vnto vs,ftretching neerer vnto her
Maiefties Dominions,then to any other part of Europe. Wee
reade that the Bees,whé they grow to be too many in their own
hiues at home, are wont to bee led out by their Captaines to
fwarme abroad, and feeke themfelues a new dwelling place.
If the examples of the Grecians and Carthaginians of olde
time,and the practife of our age may not mooue vs, yet let vs
learne wifdome of thefe fmal weake and vnreafonable creatures.
It chaunced very lately that vpon occafion I had great conference
in matters of Cofmographie with an excellent learned man of
Portingale,moft priuie to all the difcoueries of his nation, who
wondered that thofe bleffed countries,from the point of Florida Northward,were all this while vnplanted by Chriftians,pro-
tefting with great affection and zeale,that if hee were nowe as
young as I(for at this prefent hee is threefcore yeeres of age)hee
woulde fel all hee had , being a man of no fmall wealth and honour,to furnifh a conuenient number of fhips to fea for the inhabiting of thofe countries, and reducing thofe gentile people
to chriftianitie.   Moreouer hee added that Iohn Barros their
chiefe Cofmographer being moued with the like defire,was the
caufe that Brefilia was firft inhabited by the Portingales : where
they haue nine baronies or lordfhips,& thirtie engennies or fu-
ger milles, two or three hundred flaues belonging to eche myll,
with a Iudge,and other officers, & a Church: fo that euery mill
is as it were a little common wealth: and that the countrie was
firft planted by fuch men,as for fmall offences were faued from
the rope. This hee fpake not onely vnto mee and in my hearing,
but alfo in the prefence of a friend of mine, a man of great fkill in
the Mathematikes. If this mans defire might bee executed, wee
might not only for the prefent time take poffefsion of that good
land,but alfo in fhort fpace by Gods grace finde out that fhorte
and eafie paffage by the Northweft,which we haue hetherto fo
long defired,and whereof wee haue many good and more then
probable coniectures : a fewe whereof I thinke it not amiffe
heere to fet downe, although your worfhip knowe them as
well.

Marginal notes:

The fpeech of a learned Portingale.

Mafter Iohn Barros the caufe of the inhabiting of Brefilia.

well as my selfe. First therefore it is not to bee forgotten, that Sebastian Gabot wrote to master Baptista Ramusius, that he veryly beleeued that all the North part of America is diuided into Islandes. Secondly that master Iohn Verarzanus, which had been thrise on that coast, in an olde excellent mappe, which he gaue to king Henrie the eight, and is yet in the custodie of master Locke, doth so lay it out, as it is to bee seene in the mappe annexed to the end of this boke, beeing made according to Verarzanus plat.

Thirdly the story of Gil Gonsalua recorded by Franciscus Lopes de Gomara, which is saide to haue sought a passage by the Northwest, seemeth to argue and proue the same . Fourthly, in the second relation of Iaques Cartier the 11. Chapter the people of Saguinay doe testifie that vpon their coastes Westwarde there is a sea the ende whereof is vnknowne vnto them. Fiftly, in the end of that discourse is added this, as a special remembrance, to wit, that they of Canada say that it is a monethes space to saile to a lande where cinamon and cloues are growing. Sixtly, the people of Florida signified vnto Iohn Ribault (as it is expressed in his discourse heerewithall imprinted) that they might saile from the Riuer of May vnto Ceuola and the south sea through their countrie within twentie dayes . Seuenthly, the experience of captaine Frobisher on the hyther side, and Sir Fraunces Drake on the backe side of America, with the testimonie of Nicolaus and Anthonius Zeni, that Estotilanda is an Islande, doth yeelde no small hope thereof. Lastly, the iudgement of the excellent Geographer Gerardus Mercator, which his sonne Rumold Mercator my friende shewed mee in his letters, & drewe out for mee in writing, is not of wise men lightly to bee regarded. His words are these. *Magna tametsi pauca de noua* **The iudgement** *Frobisheri nauigatione scribis, quam miror ante multos annos* **of Gerardus** *nō fuisse attentatam. Non enim dubium est, quin recta & bre-* **Mercator of a** *uis via pateat in occidentem Cathaium vsq̨. In quod regnū,* **passage by the** *si recte nauigationem instituant, nobilissimas totius mundi* **Northwest.** *merces colligent, & multis Gentibus adhuc idololatris Christi nomen communicabunt.* You write (saith hee to his sonne) great matters though very briefly of the newe discouerie of Frobisher, which I wonder was neuer these many yeeres heeretofore attempted. For there is no doubt, but that there is a straight and short way open into the West euen vnto Cathay. Into which kingdome, if they take their course aright, they shall gather the most noble merchandise of all the worlde, and shall make the name of Christe to bee knowne vnto many idolatrous and Heathen people. And heere to conclude and shut vp this matter, I haue hearde my selfe of Merchants of credite that haue liued long in Spaine, that King Phillip hath made a lawe of late that none of his subiectes shall discouer to the Northwardes of fiue and fortie degrees of America : whiche may bee thought to proceede chiefly of two causes, the one, least passing farther to the North they should discouer the open passage from the south sea to our north sea : the other becaufe they haue not people enough to possesse and keepe that passage, but rather thereby shoulde open a gappe for other nations to passe that way. Certes if hetherto in our owne discoueries we had not beene led with a preposterous desire of seeking rather gaine then Gods glorie, I assure my self that our labours had taken farre better effecte. But wee forgotte, that Godlinesse is great riches, and that if we first seeke the kingdome of God, al other thinges will be giuen vnto vs, and that as the light accompanieth the Sunne, and the heate the fire, so lasting riches do waite vpon them that are zealous for the aduauncement of the kingdome of Christ, and the enlargement of his glorious Gospell : as it is sayde, I will honour them that honour mee. I truste that nowe being taught by their manifolde losses our men will take a more godly course, and vse some part of their goods to his glorie : if not, he will turne euen their couetousnes to serue him, as he hath done the pride and auarice of the Spaniardes and Portingales, who pretending in glorious words that they made their discoueries chiefly to conuert Infidelles to our most holy faith, (as they say) in deed and truth sought not them, but their goods and riches. Whiche thing that our nation may more speedily & happily performe, there is no better meane in my simple iudgement then the increase of knowledge in the arte of nauigation, &

brea

A lawe made of late by king Phillip.

Dedicatorie.

breading of skilfulnesse in the sea men: whiche Charles the Emperour and the king of Spaine that nowe is wisely considering haue in their Contractation house in Siuill appointed a learned reader of the sayde art of Nauigation, and ioyned with him certayne examiners, and haue distinguished the orders among the sea men, as the groomet whiche is the basest degree, the mariner which is the seconde, the master the thirde, and the pilote the fourth, vnto the which two last degrees none is admitted without hee haue heard the reader for a certaine space (which is commonly an excellent Mathematician, of which number were Pedro di Medina which writte learnedly of the art of nauigation, and Alonso di Chauez & Hieronimus di Chauez, whose works likewise I haue seene) and being founde fitte by him and his assistantes, which are to examine matters touching experience, they are admitted with as great solemnitie and giuing of presents to the ancient masters and Pilots, and the reader and examiners, as the great doctors in the Vniuersities, or our great Sergeantes at the law when they proceed, and so are admitted to take charge for the Indies. And that your worshippe may knowe that this is true, Master Steuen Borrows, nowe one of the foure masters of the Queenes nauie, tolde me that newely after his returne from the discouery of Moscouie by the North, in Queene Maries daies, the Spaniards, hauing intelligence that he was master in that discouerie, tooke him into their cōtractation house at their making and admitting of masters and pilots, giuing him great honour, & presented him with a payre of perfumed gloues woorth fiue or sixe Ducates. I speake all this to this ende, that the like order of erecting such a Lecture here in London or about Ratcliffe in some conuenient place, were a matter of great consequence and importance, for the sauing of many mens liues and goods, which nowe through grosse ignorance are dayly in great hazerd, to the no small detriment of the whole realme. For whiche cause I haue dealt with the right worshipfull sir Frances Drake, that seeing God hath blessed him so wonderfully, he woulde do this honour to him selfe and benefite to his countrey, to bee at the cost to erecte such a lecture : Whereunto in most bountifull maner

The side notes:

The cōtractation house at Siuill.

M. Steuen Borrowes.

A lecture of the art of nauigatiō necessarie for to be erected in London.

¶ 3   as

The bountifull offer of sir Francis Drake toward furthering the art of Nauigation.

at the verie first he answered, that he liked so well of the motion, that he woulde giue twentie poundes by the yeere standing, and twentie poundes more before hand to a learned man to furnish him with instruments and maps, that woulde take this thing vpon him: yea so readie he was that he earnestly requested mee to helpe him to the notice of a fitte man for that purpose, which I, for the zeale I bare to this good actió, did presently, & brought him one, who came vnto him & conferred with him thereupon: but in fine he would not vndertake the lecture, vnlesse he might haue fourtie pounde a yeere standing, and so the matter ceased for that time: howebeit the worthie and good Knight remaineth still constant, and will be, as he told me very lately, as good as his worde. Nowe if God shoulde put into the head of any noble man to contribute other twentie pounde, to make this lecture a competent liuing for a learned man, the whole realme no doubt might reape no small benefite thereby, To leaue this matter & to drawe to an ende, I haue heare right worshipfull in this hastie worke first put downe the title which we haue to that part of America which is from Florida to 67.degrees northwarde, by the

Ihon Gabote and his three sonnes.

letters patentes graunted to Iohn Gabote and his three sonnes, Lewes, Sebastian, and Santius, with Sebastians owne Certificate to Baptista Ramusius of his discouerie of America, and the testimonie of Fabian our own Chronicler. Next I haue caused to bee added the letters of M. Robert Thorne to King Henrie the eight, and his discourse to his Ambassadour doctor Ley in Spaine of the like argument, with the kings setting out of two ships for discouerie in the 19.yere of his raigne. Thé I haue translated the voyage of Iohn Verarzanus from thirtie degrees to Cape Briton, (& the last yeere at my charges, and other of my friendes by my exhortation, I caused Iaques Cartiers two voyages of discouering the grand Bay, and Canada, Saguinay, and Hochelaga to bee translated out of my Volumes, which are to be annexed to this present translation). Moreouer following the order of the map, and not the course of time, I haue put downe the discourse of Nicholaus and Antonius Zenie. The last treatise of Iohn Ribault, is a thing that hath been alreadie printed, but not nowe to

be

be had, vnleſſe I had cauſed it to be printed againe, The mappe
is maſter Michael Lockes, a man, for his knowledge in diuers languages and eſpecially in Coſmographie, able to doe his countrey
good, and worthie in my iudgement, for the manifolde good
partes in him, of good reputation and better fortune. This curſo-
rie pamphlet I am ouer bold to preſent vnto your worſhippe :
but I had rather want a litle diſcretion, then to bee founde vn-
thankful to him, which hath been alwaies ſo readie to pleaſure me
and all my name.

    Heere I ceaſe, crauing pardon for my ouer boldneſſe, truſt-
ing alſo that your worſhippe will continue & increaſe
your accuſtomed fauour towarde theſe
godly and honourable diſ-
coueries.

Your worſhippes humble alwayes
to commaunde, R. H.

4

A latine copie of the letters patentes
of King Henrie the seuenth, graunted
vnto Iohn Gabote and his three sonnes, Lewes,
Sebastian, and Santius for the discouering of
newe and vnknowen
landes.

ENricus dei gratia rex Angliæ
& Franciæ, & dominus hibernia,
omnibus ad quos præsentes lite=
ræ nostra peruenerint, salutem.
Notum sit & manifestum, quod
dedimus & concessimus, ac per
præsentes damus & concedimus
pro nobis & hæredibus nostris
dilectis nobis Ioanni Gaboto ci=
ui Veneciarum, Lodouico, Se-
bastiano, & Santio, filiis dicti Ioannis, & eorum & cuiuslibet e=
orum hæredibus & deputatis plenam ac liberam authoritatē,
facultatem & potestatem nauigandi ad omnes partes, regiones
& sinus maris orientalis, occidentalis, & septentrionalis sub
banneris, vexillis, & insigniis nostris, cum quinque nauibus siue
nauigiis, cuiuscunque portitura & qualitatis existant, & cum
tot et tantis nautis & hominibus, quot & quantos in dictis na=
uibus secum ducere voluerint, suis & eorum propriis sumpti=
bus & expensis, ad inueniendum, discoperiendum, & inuesti=
gandum quascunque insulas, patrias, regiones siue prouincias
gentilium & infidelium quorumcunqne in qnacunque parte
mundi positas, quæ Christianis omnibus ante hac tempora fue=
rint incognitæ. Concessimus etiam eisdem & eorum cuilibet,
eorumque & cuiuslibet eorum hæredibus & deputatis ac licen=
tiam dedimus ad affigendum prædictas banneras nostras & in=
signia in quacunque villa, oppido, castro, insula seu terra firma
a se nouiter inuentis. Et quôd prænominatus Ioannes & filii
A   eiusdem

eiusdem seu haredes & eorundem deputati, quascunq; biusmo=
di villas, castra, oppida & insulas a se inuentas, qua subiugari,
occupari, possideri possint subiugare, occupare, possidere valeat,
tanquã vasalli nostri, & gubernatores, loca tenentes & depuia=
ti, eorundem dominium, titilum, & iurisdictionem earun=
dem villarum, castrorum, oppidorum, insularum, ac terra firma
sic inuentorum nobis acquirendo. Ita tamen vt ex omnibus
fructibus, proficuis, emolumentis, commodis, lucris, & obuenti=
onibus ex huiusmodi nauigatione prouenientibus prafatus Io=
annes & filij ac haredes, & eorum deputati teneãtur & sint ob=
ligati nobis pro omni viagio suo, toties quoties ad portũ nostrũ
Bristollie applicuerint (ad quem omnino applicare teneãtur,
& sint astricti) deductis omnibus suptibus & impensis necessa=
riis per eosdem factis, quintam partem capitalis lucri facti, siue
in mercibus siue in pecuniis persoluere. Dantes nos & concedẽ=
tes eisdẽ suisq; hardibus & deputatis, vt ab omni solutione cu=
stumarum omniũ & singulorum bonorum ac mercium, quas se=
cum reportarint ab illis locis sic nouiter inuentis, liberi sint &
immunes. Et insuper dedimus & concessimus eisdem ac su=
is haredibus & deputatis, quòd terra omnes firma, iusula, vil=
la, oppida, castra, & loca quacunq; a se inuenta, quotquot ab eis
inueniri contigerit, non possint ab aliis quibusuis nostris subdi=
tis frequentari seu visitari, absq; licentia pradictorum Ioannis
& eius filiorum suorumq; deputatorum, sub pana amissionis tã
nauium, quám bonorum omniũ quorumcunq; ad ea loca sic in=
uenta nauigare prasumtiũ. Volentes & strictissimé mandan=
tes omnibus & singulis nostris subditis tam in terra quám in
mari constitutis, vt prafato Ioanni & eius filiis, ac deputatis
bonã assistentiam faciant, & tam in armandis nauibus seu na=
uigiis, quám in prouisione quietatus & victualium pro sua pe=
cunia emendorum, atq; aliarum omnium rerum sibi prouiden=
darum pro dicta nauigatione sumenda, suos omnes fauores &
auxilia impertiant . In cuius rei testimonium has literas no=
stras fieri fecimus patentes: teste me ipso apud Westmonaste=
riũ quinto die Martij, anno regni nostri vndecimo.

The:

Enrie by the grace of GOD king of England, and France, and Lorde of Irelande, to all, to whom these presentes shall come, greeting. Be it knowen that wee haue giuen and gran- ted, and by these presentes doe giue and grant for vs and our heyres, to our well beloued John Gabote citizen of Ue- nice, to Lewes, Sebastian, and Santius, sonnes of the saide John, and to the heires of them and euery of them, and their deputies, full and free authoritie, leaue, and power to sayle to all partes, countreys and seas of the East, of the West, and of the North vnder our banners and ensignes, with fiue ships, of what burden or quantitie soeuer they be: and as many ma- riners or men as they will haue with them in the saide ships, vpon their owne proper costes and charges to seeke out, dis- couer and finde whatsoeuer iles, countreyes, regions, or pro- uinces, of the heathen and infidelles whatsoeuer they bee, and in what part of the worlde soeuer they be, whiche before this time haue been vnknowen to all Christians. We haue gran- ted to them also and to euery of them, the heires of them, and euery of them and their deputies, & haue giuen them li- cence to set vp our banners and ensignes in euery village, towne, castel, yle, or maine lande of them newely founde. And that the foresaid John and his sonnes or their heires and as- signes may subdue, occupie, and possesse all such townes, ci- ties, castles and yles of them founde, which they can subdue, occupie, and possesse, as our vassailes and lieutenantes, get- ting vnto vs the rule, title, and iurisdiction of the same villa- ges, townes, castles, and firme lande so founde.

Licence graun- to John Gabot, his sonnes and heires, to disco- uer vnknowen landes vnder the kings banner.

To subdue and possesse those landes as the kings vassalles.

A 2   Yet

Yet so that the foresaide John and his sonnes and heires, and their Deputies bee holden and bounden, of all the fruites, profites, gaines & commodities growing of such nauigation, for euery their voyage as often as they shall arriue at our port of Bristoll, (at the which port they shall be bounde and holden only to arriue) all manner of necessarie costes and charges by them made being deducted, to pay vnto vs

The fift of all goods to be paid to the king.

in wares or money the fifth part of the Capitall gaine so gotten . Wee giuing and graunting vnto them and to their heires and Deputies, that they shall bee free from all

Freedome from all customes.

paying of customes of all and singuler such merchandize, as they shall bring with them from those places so newely founde.

And moreouer wee haue giuen and graunted to them, their heires and Deputies, that all the firme landes, Iles, Uillages, Townes, Castles and places whatsoeuer they

None but they & their assignes may trauaile thither.

be, that they shall chaunce to finde, may not of any other of our subiectes bee frequented or visited without the licence of the foresayd John, his sonnes and their deputies vnder paine of forfayture as well of their shippes, as of all and singuler goods of all them that shall presume to sayle to those places so founde. Willing and most straightly commaunding all and singuler our subiectes as well on lande as on sea appointed officers, to giue good assistance to the aforesaid John and his sonnes and deputies, and that as well in arming and furnishing their ships or vessels, as in prouision of quietnesse, and in buying of victualles for their money and all other thinges by them to be prouided necessarie for the saide nauigation, they doe giue them all their helpe and fauour. In witnesse whereof wee haue caused to bee made these our let-

The 5. of march 1594.

ters patentes. Witnesse our selfe at Westminster the fift day of March in the xi. yeere of our reigne.

¶ A

❧ A note of Sebaſtian Gabotes
voyage of diſcouerie, taken out of an old
Chronicle written by Robert Fabian ſomtime
Alderman of London, which is in the cuſtodie of
Iohn Stowe Citizen, a diligent ſearcher
and preſeruer of Antiquities.

THIS yeere the King, (by In the 13. yeere of king Henrie the vij. 1498. meanes of a Uenetian whiche made himſelfe very expert and cunning in knoweledge of the circuite of the worlde and Iſlandes of the ſame, as by a Carde and other demonſtrations reaſonable hee ſhewed) cauſed to man and victuall a ſhippe at Briſtowe, to ſearche Note. for an Iſlande, whiche, hee ſaide hee knewe well, was riche and repleniſhed with riche commodities. Which Ship thus manned and victualed at the kinges coſt, diuers merchants of London ventured in her ſmall ſtockes, being in her as chiefe Patrone the ſaide Uenetian. And in the companie of the ſaide ſhippe ſayled alſo out of Briſtowe three or Briſtow. foure ſmall ſhips fraught with ſleight and groſſe merchandizes, as courſe cloth, Caps, Laces, points and other trifles, and ſo departed from Briſtowe in the beginning of May: William Purchas Maior of London. of whome in this Maiors time returned no tidings.

Of three ſauage men which hee brought home, and preſented vnto the king in the xvii. yeere of his raigne.

THis yeere alſo were brought vnto the king three men Three ſauage men brought in into England. taken in the new founde Iland, that before I ſpake of

Rawe flesh.
Beastes skins.

in William Purchas time being Maior. These were clothed in beastes skinnes, and ate rawe fleshe, and spake such
speech that no man coulde vnderstand them, and in their be-
meanour like to bruite beastes, whom the king kept a time
after. Of the which vpon two yeeres past after J saw two
apparelled after the maner of Englishe men in Westminster pallace, which at that time J coulde not discerne from
Englishe men, till J was learned what they were. But as
for speech J heard none of them vtter one worde.

Iohn Baptista Ramusius in his Preface to the thirde
volume of the nauigations, writeth thus of
Sebastian Gabot.

IN the latter part of this volume are put certaine relations of Iohn de Uerarzana a Florentine, and of a great
Captaine a Frenchman, and the two voyages of Iaques
Cartier a Briton, who sailed vnto the lande set in fiftie degrees of latitude to the north, which is called New France:
of the which landes hitherto it is not throughly knowne
whether they doe ioyne with the firme lande of Florida and
nova Hispania, or whether they be separated & diuided all by
Sebastian
Gabots letters
to Ramusius.
the Sea as Ilands : and whether that by that way one may
goe by Sea vnto the countrie of Cathaio : as many yeeres
past it was written vnto me by Sebastian Gaboto our countrie man Uenetian, a man of great experience & very rare
in the art of Nauigation, and the knowledge of Cosmographie : who sayled along and beyonde this land of Newe
Note.
Fraunce at the charges of king Henrie the seuenth king of
He calleth them
Ilands.
Englande : And hee tolde mee that hauing sayled a long
time West and by North beyonde these Ilandes vnto the
latitude of 67. degrees and an halfe vnder the North Pole,
and at the 11. day of Iune finding still the open Sea
Sebastian
Gabot might
haue sailed to
Cathaio.
without any maner of impediment, hee thought verily by
that way to haue passed on still the way to Cathaio, which is
in the East, and woulde haue done it, if the mutinie of the
shipmaster

shipmaster and marriners had not rebelled and made him to returne homewardes from that place. But it seemeth that God doth yet still reserue this great enterprise for some great Prince, to discouer this voyage of Cathaio by this way: which for the bringing of the spiceries from India into Europe were the most easie and shortest of all other wayes hetherto founde out. And surely this enterprise woulde bee the most glorious and of most importance of all other that can be imagined, to make his name great, & fame immortall to all ages to come, farre more then can bee done by any of all these great troubles and warres, which dayly are vsed in Europe among the miserable Christian people.

This voyage to Cathay reserued by God for some great Prince.

This way the shortest of all others.

This discouery were a most glorious enterprise.

This much concerning Sebastian Gabotes discouerie may suffice for a present tast: but shortly, God willing, shall come out in print all his owne mappes & discourses drawne and written by himselfe, which are in the custodie of the worshipfull master William Worthington one of her Maiesties Pensioners, who (because so worthie monumentes shoulde not be buried in perpetuall obliuion) is very willing to suffer them to be ouerseene and published in as good order as may bee, to the encouragement and benefite of our Countriemen.

William Worthington Pensioner.

A declaration of the Indies and landes

discouered, and subdued vnto the Emperour, and the king
of Portugale. And also of other partes of the Indies
and rich Conntries to bee discouered, which the worshipfull master Robert Thorne merchant of London (who dwelt long in the City of Siuil in
Spaine) exhorted king Henrie the eight
to take in hande.

MOST EXCELLENT PRINCE.

Experience proueth that naturallly all Princes bee desirous to extend and enlarge their dominions and kingdomes. Wherfore it is not to bee maruelled, to see them euery day procure ẙ same, not regarding any cost, perill, and labour, that may thereby chaunce, but rather it is to bee maruelled, if there be any prince content to liue quiet with his owne dominions. For surely the people would thinke he lacketh the noble courage and spirit of all other. The worlde knoweth that the desires of Princes haue beene so feruent to obtaine their purpose, that they haue aduentured and proued things to mans coniecture impossible, the which they haue made possible, and also things difficult haue made facil, and thus to obtaine their purpose haue in maner turned vp and downe the whole worlde so many times, that the people inhabiting in the farthest regiõ of the occident haue pursued with great desires, labours and perils, to penetrate and enter into the farthest regions of the Orient: And in likewise those people of the said partes of the Orient haue had no lesse labour and desire to enter and penetrate into the farthest land of the Occident, and so following their purchase haue not seased vntill they

could

coulo paſſe no farther by reaſon of the great Seas. ¶ This
naturall inclination is cauſe, that ſcarſely it may bee ſaide
there is any kingdome ſtable, nor king quiet, but that his
owne imagination, or other Princes his neighbours doe
trouble him. God and nature hath prouided to your Grace,
and to your Gracious progenitors this Realme of Englande, and ſet it in ſo fruitefull a place, and within ſuche limites, that it ſhoulde ſeeme to bee a place quiet and aparted
from all the foreſaide deſires. One ſpeciall cauſe is, for
that it is compaſſed with the Sea : by reaſon thereof it
ſeemes, this notwithſtanding, their deſires and noble cou-
rages haue been moſt commonly like vnto others : and with
maruellous great labours, coſtes and perilles, they haue tra-
uelled and paſſed the Seas making warre not onely with
kings and dominions nigh neighbours, but alſo with them
of farre countries, and ſo hath wonne and conquered many
riche and faire Dominions, and amplified this your Graces
Realme with great victorie and glory. And alſo nowe of
late your Grace hauing like courage and deſire, & not without iuſt cauſe, to enlarge this your kingdome and demaund
your limites and tribute of the French king, which at that
preſent hee reſtrained your Grace in perſon paſſed with a
great power into France, putting your Graces perſon to
great paine and labour, and without doubt victoriouſly you
had conquered the ſaide Realme of Fraunce, as yee began,
if your aduerſarie had not reconciled him, and knowledged
your Graces right and title : and ſo promiſed truely to pay
the tribute then due, and fulfill your requeſt in all thinges,
and alſo deſired your Grace for peace, the which of your cle-
mencie you could not refuſe.

Nowe I conſidering this your noble courage and
deſire, & alſo perceiuing that your Grace may at your pleaſure, to your greater glory, by a godly meane, with litle coſt,
perill, or labour to your Grace or any of your Subiectes,
amplifie and inriche this your ſaide Realme, I knowe it is
my bounde dutie to manifeſt this ſecrete vnto your Grace,
which

which hitherto as I suppose hath beene hid : which is that Note.
with a small number of shippes there may bee discouered
diuers newe landes and kingdomes, in the whiche without
doubt your Grace shall winne perpetuall glory and your
Subiects infinite profite.   To which places there is
left one way to discouer, which is into the North : For that
of the foure parts of the worlde it seemeth three partes are
discouered by other Princes .   For out of Spaine they
haue discouered all the Indies and Seas Occidentall, and
out of Portugale all the Indies and Seas Oriental : So
that by this part of the Orient and Occident, they haue
compassed the worlde .   For the one of them departing towarde the Orient, and the other towarde the Occident, met
againe in the course or way of the middest of the day, and
so then was discouered a great part of the same Seas and
coastes by the Spaniardes. So that nowe rest to bee discouered the saide North partes, the which it seemeth to
mee, is onely your charge and duetie.   Because the situation of this your Realme is thereunto neerest and ap-
test of all other : and also for that you haue alreadie taken Note.
it in hande : And in mine opinion, it will not seeme well
to leaue so great and profitable an enterprise, seeing it may
so easily and with so little coste, labour, and daunger,
bee followed and obteined : Though heeretofore your
Grace hath made theereof a proofe, and founde not the
commoditie thereby as you trusted, at this time it shall
bee no impediment.   For there may bee nowe prouided
remedies for thinges , then lacked, and the inconueniences and lettes remooued that then were cause your Graces desire tooke no full effect , which is, the courses to be
chaunged, and followe the aforesaid new courses. And concerning the marriners, shippes, and prouision, an order may
be deuised and taken meete and conuenient much better then
hetherto. By reason whereof, and by Gods grace, no doubt
your purpose shall take effect. Surely the coste heerein
will bee nothing , in comparison to the great profite.

The labour is much lesse, yea nothing at all, where so great honour and glory is hoped for : and considering well the courses, truly the danger & way is shorter to vs, then to Spaine or Portugall, as by euident reasons appeareth . And nowe to declare some thing of the commoditie and vtilitie of this Nauigation and discouering, it is very cleere and certaine, that the Seas that commonly men say, that without great danger, difficultie and perill, yea rather it is impossible to passe, those same Seas bee nauigable and without any such daunger, but that shippes may passe and haue in them perpetuall cleerenesse of the day without any darkenesse of the night : which thing is a great commoditie for the nauigants, to see at all times rounde about them, as well the safegardes as daungers, and howe great difference it is betweene the commoditie and perilles of other which leaue the most parte of euery foure and twentie houres the saide light, and goe in darkenesse groping their way , I thincke there is none so ignorant but perceiueth this more plainely, then it can bee expressed : yea what a vantage shall your Graces Subiects haue also by this light to discouer the strange landes , countries, and coastes, for if they that bee discouered to sayle by them in darkenesse is with great danger, muche more then the coastes not discouered be dangerous to trauell by night or in darkenesse. Yet these dangers or darknesse hath not letted the Spaniardes and Portingals and other, to discouer many vnknowen realmes to their great perill, which considered (and that your Graces Subiectes maye haue the saide lighte) it will seeme your Graces subiects to bee without actiuitie or courage, in leauing to doe this glorious and noble enterprise . For they being past this little way which they named so dangerous, which may bee ii, or iii. leagues before they come to ȳ Pole, and as much more after they passe the Pole, it is cleere that from thence foorth the Seas and landes are as temperat as in these partes, & that then it may be at the will and pleasure of the marriners, to choose whether they will saile by ȳ

coastes

coaſtes that bee colde,temperate,oʒ hot. Foʒ they being paſt
the pole,it is plaine they maye decline to what parte they
liſt.If they will goe towarde the Oʒient they ſhall inioy the
regions of all the Tartarians that extende towarde the mid-
day,and from thence they may goe and pʒoceede to the lande
of ꝑ Chinas,& from thence to the lande of Cathaio oʒiental,
which is of all the mayne lande moſt oʒientall that can bee
reckoned from our habitation. And if from thence they doe
continue their nauigation,following the coaſte that returns
towarde the occident,they ſhall fall in Melaſſa,and ſo in all
the Indees which we call oʒientall, and following that way
may returne hither by the Cape of Bona Speranſa:and thus
they ſhall compaſſe the whole woʒlde. And if they will take
their courſe after they be paſt the pole, towarde the occident,
they ſhall goe in the backe ſide of the new found lande,which
of late was diſcouered by your Graces ſubiectes, vntill they
come to the backſide and South ſeas of the Indees occi-
dentalls. And ſo continuing their viage they may returne
thoʒowe the ſtraite of Magallanas to this countrey, and ſo
they compaſſe alſo the woʒlde by that way , and if they goe
this thirde way,and after they bee paſt the pole,goe right towarde the pole Antartike,and then decline toward the lands
and Ilands ſituated betweene the Tropikes , and vnder the
Equinoctial,without doubt they ſhal find there ꝑ richeſt lāds
and Ilands of the woʒlde of Golde,pʒecious ſtones, balmes,
ſpices, and other thinges that wee here eſteeme moſt : which
come out of ſtrang countreys,& may returne the ſame way.

By this it appeareth your Grace haue not onely a greate
aduantage of the riches , but alſo your ſubiectes ſhal not trauell halfe of the way that other doe, which goe rounde a-
bout as afoʒeſaide.

The booke made by the right worship-
full Master Robert Thorne in the yeere 1527. in Siuill to Doctour ley, Lorde ambassadour for King Hen
rie the eight to Charles the Emperour, being an
information of the parts of the world, discouered by him and the King of Portingale: And also of the way to the
Moluccaes by the
north,

Ight noble & reuerende in &c.
I receiued your letters, & haue
procured and sent to knowe of
your seruant, who your Lorde-
ship wrote shoulde bee sicke in
Merchena. I can not there or
els where heare of him, wout
he be returned to you, or gone
to S. Lucar & shipt. I can not
iudge but that of some contagi-
ous sicknes he died, so that the owner of the house for defa-
ming his house woulde bury him secretly, and not be known
of it. For such things haue ofte times happened in this countrey.

Also to write to your Lordshippe of the newe trade
of spicerie of the Emperour, there is no doubt but that the I-
landes are fertile of cloues, nutmegs, mace, and cinnamon:
And that the saide Ilandes, with other there about, abounde
wh gold, Rubies, Diamonds, Balasses, Granates, iacincts &
other stones & pearles, as al other lāds, that are vnder & nere
ye equinoctial. For we see, where nature giueth any thing, she
is no nigarde. For as with vs and other, that are aparted
from the sayde equinoctiall, our mettalles be lead, tynne, and
yron, so theirs be golde, siluer, and copper. And as our
fruites and graines be aples, nuttes, and corne, so theirs bee
dates, nutmegges, pepper, cloues, and other spices. And as
wee

wee haue iette, amber, criftall, iafper, and other like ſtones, ſo haue they rubies, diamonds, balaſſes, ſaphires, Iacincts, and other like. And though ſome ſay that of ſuch precious mettals, graines or kind of ſpices, and precious ſtones, the abboundance and quantitie is nothing ſo great, as our mettals, fruites or ſtones aboue rehearſed: yet if it be well confidered, how the quantitie of the earth vnder the equinoctiall to both the tropicall lines, (in which ſpace is founde the ſaid golde, ſpices and precious ſtones) to be as much in quantitle, as almoſt all the earth from the tropickes to both the poles: it can not be denied but there is more quantitie of the ſaid mettels, fruites, ſpices, and precious ſtones, then there is of the other mettels and other thinges before rehearſed. And I ſee that the preciouſneſſe of theſe thinges is meaſured after the diſtance that is betweene vs, and the things that we haue appetite vnto. For in this nauigation of the ſpicerie was diſcouered, that theſe Ilandes nothing ſet by golde, but ſet more by a knife and a nayle of yron, then by his quantitie of Golde: and with reaſon, as the thing more neceſſarie for mans ſeruice. And I doubt not but to them ſhoulde bee as precious our corne and ſeedes, if they might haue them, as to vs their ſpices: and likewiſe the peeces of glaſſe that heare wee haue counterfayted are as precious to them, as to vs their ſtones: which by experience is ſeene daylie by them that haue trade thither. This of the riches of thoſe countries is ſufficient.

Touching that your Lordſhip wrote, whether it may be profitable to the Emperour or no, it may be without doubte of great profit: if as the king of Portingall doth, he woulde become a marchant, and prouide ſhippes and their lading, and trade thither alone, and defende the trade of theſe Ilands for himſelfe. But other greater buſineſ withholdeth him from this. But ſtill, as nowe it is begunne to bee occupied, it woulde come to much. For the ſhips comming in ſafetie, there woulde thither many euery yeere, of whiche to the Emperour is due of all the wares and Iuelles that come from

thence the fift part for his cuſtome cleare without any coſt.
And beſides this he putteth in euery flote a certayn quantitie
of money, of whiche hee enioyeth of the gaines pounde and
poundes like as other aduenturers doe. In a flote of three
ſhippes and a carauell that went from this citie armed by
the marchauntes of it, which departed in Aprill laſt paſt, I
and my partener haue 1400. Ducates that we employed in
the ſayde fleete, principally for that two Engliſhmen friends

Note.

of mine, whiche are ſomewhat learned in Coſinographie,
ſhoulde goe in the ſame ſhippes, to bring mee certaine relation of the ſituation of the countrey, and to bee experte in the
Nauigation of thoſe ſeas, and there to haue informations of
many other things, and aduiſe that I deſire to know eſpecially. Seeing in theſe quarters are ſhippes, and marriners of
that countrey, and cardes by which they ſayle, though much
vnlike ours: that they ſhould procure to haue the ſaid Cards,
and learne howe they vnderſtande them, and eſpecially to
know what Nauigation they haue for thoſe Ilandes Northwardes, and Northeaſtwarde.

Note.

For if from the ſayde Ilandes the Sea do extende, without
interpoſition of lande, to ſayle from the North poynt
to the Northeaſt poynt 1700, or 1800. leagues, they ſhould
come to the Newe founde Ilandes that wee diſcouered, and
ſo wee ſhoulde bee neerer to the ſayde ſpicerie by almoſt
2000, leagues then the Emperour, or the king of Portingal
are. And to aduiſe your Lordſhippe whether of theſe ſpiceries of the King of Portingal or the Emperours is neerer,
and alſo of the titles that eyther of them hath, and howe
our Newe founde landes are parted from it, (for that by
writyng without ſome demonſtration, it were harde to giue
any declaration of it,)   I haue cauſed that your Lorde-
ſhippe ſhall receyue herewith a little Mappe or Carde of
the worlde : the whiche, I feare mee, ſhall put your Lordſhippe to more labour to vnderſtande, then mee to make
it, only for that it is made in ſo little roome that it cannot be
but obſcurely ſet out, ꝑ is deſired to be ſeene in it, & alſo for
ꝑ I am in this ſcience litle expert: Yet to remedy in part this
difficul-

difficultie, it is necessary to declare to your Lordshippe my intent, with which I trust you shal perceiue in this card part of your desire, if, for that I cannot expresse mine intent, with my declaratiō I doe not make it more obscure.

First, your Lordship knoweth that the Cosmographers haue deuided the earth by 360. degrees in latitude, and as many in longitude, vnder the which is comprehended al the roundnesse of the earth: the latitude beeing deuided into 4. quarters, ninetie degrees amount to euerie quarter, which they measure by the altitude of the poles, that is the North and South starres, beeing from the line equinoctiall till they come right vnder the Noth starre the saide ninetie degrees: and asmuche from the sayde line equinoctiall to the South starre bee other ninetie degrees. And asmuche more is also from eyther of the saide starres agayne to the equinoctiall. Which imagined to be rounde, is soone perceiued thus, 360. degrees of latitude to be consumed in the said foure quarters, of ninetie degrees a quarter, so that this latitude is the measure of the worlde from North to South, and from South to North. And the longitude, in which are also counted other 360. is counted frō West to East, or from East to West, as in the card is set. The said latitude your Lordship may see marked and deuided in the end of this carde on the left hande. So that if you woulde To know the latitudes. know in what degrees of latitude any region or coast standeth, take a compasse and set the one foote of the same in the equinoctiall line right against the said region, and apply the other foote of the compasse to the saide region or coast, and then set the sayd compasse at the ende of the carde, where the degrees are deuided. And the one foote of the cōpasse standing in the line equinoctiall, the other will shewe in the scale the degrees of altitude or latitude that the sayd region is in. Also the longitude of the worlde I haue set out in the nether part of the carde, contayning also 360. degrees: which begin to be coūted after Ptolome and other Cosmographers from an head land called *Capo verde*, which is ouer against a little crosse made in the part occidentall, where

℃   the

the diuision of the degrees beginneth, & endeth in ye same *Capo verde*. Nowe to knowe in what longitude any lande is, your Lordeshippe muſt take a ruler or a compaſſe, and ſet the one foote of the compaſſe vpon the lande or coaſt whoſe longitude you woulde knowe, and extende the other foote of the compaſſe to the nexte parte of one of the tranſuerſall lines in the Orientall or Occidentall part: which done, ſet the one foote of the compaſſe in the ſaide tranſuerſall lyne at the ende of the nether ſcale, the ſcale of longitude, and the other foote ſheweth the degree of longitude that the region is in. And your Lordſhippe muſt vnderſtande that this carde though little conteyneth the vniuerſall whole worlde betwixte the twoo collaterall lines, the one in the Occidentall parte deſcendeth perpendicular vppon the 175. degree, and the other in the Orientall on the 170. degree, whoſe diſtaunce meaſureth the ſcale of longitude. And that whiche is without the two ſayde tranſuerſall lynes is onely to ſhew howe the Oriental part is ioyned with the Occident, & Occident with the Orient. For that that is ſet without the line in the Orient parte, is the ſame that is ſet within the other line in the Occidentall parte: and againe that that is ſette without the line in the Occidentall part, is the ſame that is ſet within the line on the Orientall parte: To ſhewe that though this figure of the worlde in playne or flat ſeemeth to haue an ende, yet one imagining that this ſayde carde were ſet vpon a round thing, where the endes ſhoulde touche by the lines, it would plainely appeare howe the Orient part ioyneth with the Occident, as there without the lines it is deſcribed & figured. And for more declaration of the ſaid card, your Lordſhip ſhall vnderſtand, that beginning on the parte Occidentall within the lyne, the firſt land that is ſet out, is ye mayne land & Iland of the Indies of ye Emperour. Which mayne lande or coaſt goeth Northwarde, and finiſheth in the lande that wee founde, whiche is called heere *Terra de Labrador*. So that it appeareth the ſayde lande that we e founde and the Indies to bee all one mayne lande. The

ſayd

sayd coast from the saide Indies Southwarde, as by the carde your Lordshippe may see, cōmeth to a certaine straite sea called *Estrecho de todos Sanctos*: by which straite Sea the Spaniardes goe to the spiceries, as I shall declare more at large: the which straite sea is right against the three hundred fifteene degrees of Longitude, and is of Latitude or altitude from the Equinoctiall fiftie three degrees. The first lande from the sayd beginning of the carde towarde the Orient is certaine Ilandes of the Canaries & Ilandes of *Capo verde*. But the first mayne lande next to the line Equinoctiall is the sayde *Capo verde*, and from thence northwarde by the streite of this sea of Italie. And so followeth Spayne, Fraunce, Flaunders, Almaine, Denmarke and Norway, which is the highest parte toward the North. And ouer against Flaunders are our Ilands of England and Irelande. Of the landes and coastes within the straites I haue set out onelye the Regions, deuiding them by lynes of their lymittes, by whiche playnelie I thinke your Lordship may see, in what situatiō euery region is, and of what highnesse, & with what regions it is ioyned. I doe thinke few are lefte out of all Europe. In the partes of Asia and Affrica I could not so well make the said diuisions: for that they be not so well knowen, nor neede not so muche. This I write because in the sayde carde bee made the sayde lynes and strikes, that your Lordshippe shoulb vnderstande wherefore they doe serue. Also returning to foresayde *Capo verde* the coast goeth Southwarde to a cape called *Capo de bona speransa*: which is right ouer agaynst the sixtye and sixtie fifte degree of Longitude. And by this cape goe the Portingales to their spicerie. For from this cape towarde the Orient, is the Lande of Calicut, as your Lordshippe may see in the head lande ouer against the 130. degree. From the said cape of *Bona Speransa* the coast returneth toward the line Equinoctiall, and passing foorth entreth the read sea, & returning out entreth againe into the gulfe of Persia, and returneth towarde the Equinoctiall line, till that it commeth to the head-

Now called the streit of Magelane.

C 2   land

land called Callicut aforesaide, and from thence the coast making a Gulfe, where is the riuer of Ganges, returneth towarde the line to a head lande called Malacha, where is the principall spicerie: And from this cape returneth and maketh a great gulfe, and after the coast goeth right toward the Orient, and ouer against this last gulfe and coast be manie Ilandes, which be Ilandes of the spiceries of the Emperour. Upon which the Portingales and he be at vartaunce.

Note.

The said coast goeth towarde the Orient, and endeth right against the 155.degrees, and after returneth toward the occident Northwarde: which coast not yet plainely knowne I may ioyn to the new found land found by vs, that I spake of before. So that I finishe with this a briefe declaration of the carde aforesayde. Well I knowe I shoulde also haue declared how the coastes within the streites of the Sea of Italie runne. It is plaine that passing the streites on the Northside of that Sea after the coast of Granado, and with that which pertaynes to Spayne, is the coast of that which Fraunce hath in Italie. And then followeth in one peece all Italie, which lande hath an arme of a sea with a gulfe which is called *Mare Adriaticum*. And in the bottome of this gulfe is the citie of Uenice. And on the other part of the said gulfe is Sclauonia, and nexte Grecia, then the streites of Constantinople, and then the Sea called *Euximus*, which is within the saide streites: And comming out of the said straits floweth toward Turcia maior. (Though now on both sides it is called Turcia.) And so the coast runneth Southward to Syria, and ouer against the said Turcia are the Ilades of Rhodes, Candie, and Cyprus. And ouer against Italie are the Ilandes of Sicilia & Sardinia. And ouer against Spaine is Maiorca and minorca. In the ende of the gulfe of Syria is Iudea. And from thence returneth the coast toward the Occident, till it commeth to the streites where wee beganne, whiche all is the coast of Affricke or Barbarie. Also your Lordshippe shall vnderstande that the coastes of the Sea throughout all the worlde I haue coloured with yellow, for that it may appeare

that

that all that is within the line coloured yellow, is to be ima=
gined to be mayne land o2 Jland: and all without the sayde
line so coloured to bee Sea: whereby it is easie and light to
know it. Albeit in this little roome any other description
would rather haue made it obscure then cleere. Also the sayd
coasts of the Sea are all set iustly after the manner & forme
as they lye, as the nauigation app2ooueth thē th2oughout all
the carde, saue onely the coastes and Jles of the spicerie of ỹ
Emperour which is from ouer against the 160. to the 215.
degrees of Longitude. Fo2 these coastes & situations of the
Jlands euery of the Cosmographers and pilots of Po2tin=
gall and Spayne doe set after their purpose. The Spani=
ards mo2e towards the O2ient, because they should appeare
to appertaine to the Emperour: and the Po2tingalles mo2e
toward the Occident, fo2 that they should fall within their
iurisdiction. So that the Pilots & nauigants thither, which
in such cases should declare ỹ truth, by their industrie doe set
thē falsely euery one to fauour his p2ince. And fo2 this cause
can be no certaine situatiō of ỹ coast & Jlands, til this diffe=
rence betwixte them be verified . Nowe to come to the
purpose of your Lo2dshippes demaunde touching the diffe=
rence betweene the Emperour and the king of Po2tingall,
to vnderstād it better, J must declare ỹ beginning of this dis=
couering. Though peraduēture your Lo2dship may say ỹ in
that J haue w2ittē ought of purpose J fall in the P2ouerbe,
A gemino ouo bellum: But your Lo2dship commaunded me
to be large, & J take licence to be p2olixouse, & shalbe perad=
uenture tedious, but your Lo2dship knoweth that *nihil igno=
rantia verbosius*. Jn the peere 1484. the king of Po2tingal
minded to arme certaine caruelles to discouer this spicery.
Then fo2asmuch as he feared that being discouered euerie
other p2ince would send & trade thither, so ỹ the cost & peril
of discouering should be his, & the p2ofite common : where=
fo2e first he gaue knowledge of this his mynd to al p2inces
ch2istened, saying ỹ he would seeke amōgst ỹ infidels newe
possessiōs of regions, & therfo2e would make a certain army:
& ỹ if any of thē would help in ỹ cost of ỹ said army he should

enioy his parte of the profite or honour that shoulde come
of it . And as then this discouering was holden for a
straunge thing and vncertaine. Nowe they say, that all the
Princes of Christendome aunsweared that they woulde bee
no part of such an army, nor yet of the profite ý might come
of it. After the which he gaue knowledge to the Pope of his
purpose, & of the answere of all the Princes, desiring him ý
seeing that none would helpe in the costes , that hee woulde
iudge all that shoulde bee founde and discouered to be of his
iurisdiction, and commaund that none other Princes should
intermeddle therewith. The Pope saide not as Christ saith,
Quis me constituit iudicem inter vos? He did not refuse, but
making him selfe as Lorde and Iudge of all, not only graū-
ted that all that should be discouered from Oriēt to Occidēt
should be the kings of Portingall, but also, that vpon great
censures no other Prince should discouer but he: And if they
did, all to be the kinges of Portingall. So he armed a fleete,
and in the yeere 1487, was discouered ý Ilands of Calicut,
from whence is brought all the spice he hath. After this in
the yeere 1492, the king of Spaine willing to discouer
landes towarde the Occident without making any such diligence, or taking licence of the king of Portingale, armed
certayne caruelles, and then discouered this India Occidentall, especially two Ilandes of the saide India, that in this
carde I set foorth named the one *Ladominica*, and the other
Cuba, and brought certaine gold from thence. Of the which
when the king of Portingall had knowledge, he sent to the
king of Spayne, requiring him to giue him ý said Ilands.
For that by the sentence of the Pope all that should be discouered was his, and that he should not proceede further in the
discouerie without his licence. And at the same time it seemeth that out of Castill, into Portingale had gone for feare
of burning infinite number of Iewes that were expelled out
of Spayne, for that they would not turne to be Christians, &
carried with thē infinite number of gold & siluer. So that it
seemeth that the king of Spayne answered that it was reasō
that the king of Portingall asked , and that to bee obedient

to

that which the pope had decreed, he would giue him the said
Ilands of the Indies. Now for as much as it was decreed
betwixt þ said kings, þ none should receiue þ others subiects
fugitiues, nor their goodes, therefore the king of Portingale
should pay and returne to the king of Spaine a million of
Golde or more, that the Iewes had carried out of Spaine to
Portingale; and that so doing he would giue these Ilandes
and desist from any more discouering. And not fulfilling this
he would not onely not giue these Ilands, but procure to
discouer more where him thought best. It seemeth that the
king of Portingale would not or could not with his ease
pay this mony. And so not paying that he coulde not let the
king of Spaine to discouer: so that hee enterprised not toward the Orient where he had begun and found the spicery.
And consented to the king of Spaine that touching this discouering they should deuide the worlde betweene them two.
And that all that should be discouered fro̅ *Capo verde*, where
this carde beginneth to be counted in the degrees of longitude, to 180, of the sayde scale of longitude, which is halfe
the worlde toward the Orient, and finisheth in this carde
right ouer against a little crosse made at the sayde 180, degrees, to be the king of Portingalles. And all the lande
from the sayde Crosse towarde the Occident, vntill it
ioyneth with the other Crosse in the Orient, which contei-
neth the other hundreth and eightie degrees, that is the
other halfe of the worlde, to bee the king of Spaynes.
So that from the lande ouer agaynst the sayde hundreth
and eightie degrees vntill it finish in the three hundred and
sixtie on both the endes of the carde, is the iurisdiction of the king of Spayne. So after this manner they
deuided the worlde betweene them. Nowe for that these
Ilandes of spicerie fall neere the terme and lymites betweene these Princes (for as by the sayde carde you maye
see they beginne from one hundred and sixtie degrees of
Longitude, and ende in 215.) it seemeth all that falleth
from 160, to 180, degrees, shoulde bee of Portingall:
and

and all the rest of Spayne. And for that their Cosmographers and Pilots could not agree in the situation of the said Ilands (for the Portingals set them al within their 180. degrees, and the Spaniards set them all without: & for that in measuring, all the Cosmographers of both partes, or

what other that euer haue beene cānot giue certaine order to measure ŷ longitude of the world, as they do of ŷ latitude: for ŷ there is no starre fixed frō East to West, as are ŷ starrs of the poles from North to South, but all mooueth with the mouing diuine:) no maner can be found how certainely it may be measured, but by coniectures, as the Nauigantes haue esteemed the way they haue gone. But it is manifest that Spayne had the situation of all the landes from *Capo verde*, towarde the Orient of the Portingales to their 180. degrees. And in all their cardes they neuer hitherto set the sayd Ilands within their limitatiō of the sayd 180. degrees: (Though they knew very well of the Ilandes,) til nowe that the Spaniards discouered them. And it is knowne that the king of Portingale had trade to these Ilands afore, but would neuer suffer Portingale to goe thither from Calicut: for so much as hee knewe that it fell out of his dominion: least by going thither there might come some knowledge of those other Ilandes of the king of Spayne, but bought the cloues of Merchauntes of that countrie, that brought them to Calicut, much deerer then they would haue cost, if he had set for thē, thinking after this maner it would abide alwaies secrete. And now that it is discouered he sendes and keepes the Spaniers from the trade all that he can. Also it should seeme that when this foresaide consent of the diuision of the worlde was agreed of betweene them, the king of Portingale had alreadye discouered certayne Ilandes that lye ouer against *Capo verde*, and also certayne parte of the mayne lande of India towarde the South, from whence he set Brasill, and called it the lande of Brasill. So for that all shoulde come in his terme and limites, hee tooke three hundred and seuentie leagues beyonde

Ca-

The longitudes harde to be founde out.

Capo verde : and after this, his 180.degrees, being his part of the woꝛlde, shoulde beginne in the Carde right ouer a-gainst the 340 degrees, where I haue made a little com-passe with a crosse, and shoulde finishe at the 160.degree, where also I haue made an other little marke. And after this computation without any controuersie, the Jlandes of the spicerie fall out of the Poꝛtingales domination. So that nowe the Spaniardes say to the Poꝛtingales that if they woulde beginne their 180. degrees from the saide Capo verde, to the intent they shoulde extende moꝛe towarde the o-riente, and so to touche those Jlandes of the spicerie of the Emperour, which is all that is betweene the two crosses made in this carde, that then the Jlandes of Capo verde and the lande of Bꝛasill that the Poꝛtingales nowe obtaine, is out of the sayde limitation, and that they are of the Empe-rours. Oꝛ if their 180. degrees they count from the 370. leagues beyonde the sayde Capo verde, to inclube in it the sayde Jlandes and landes of Bꝛasill, then plainely appea-reth the saide 180. degrees shoulde finishe longe befoꝛe they come to these Jlandes of the spicerie of the Emperour : As by this Carde your Loꝛdeshippe may see. Foꝛ their li-mittes shoulde beginne at the 340. degrees, of this Carde, and ende at 160.degrees, where I haue made two little marks of the compasse with crosses in them.

So that plainely it shoulde appeare by reason, that the Poꝛtingales shoulde leaue these Jlandes of Capo verde and land of Bꝛasill, if they would haue part of the spicerie of the Emperours: oꝛ else holding these, they haue no parte there. To this the Poꝛtingales say, that they will beginne their 180. degrees from the selfe same Capo verde : foꝛ that it maye extende so muche moꝛe towarde the oꝛiente and touche these Jlandes of the Emperours : and woulde winne these Jlandes of Capo verde and lande of Bꝛasill ne-uer the lesse, as a thinge that they possessed befoꝛe the con-sent of this limitation was made.

So none can verylye tell whiche hath the best reason.

They

D.

They bee not yet agreed, Quæd sub Iudice lis est)
But without doubte by all coniectures of reason the sayde
Ilandes fall all without the limitation of Portingale, and
pertayne to Spaine, as it appeareth by the most parte of all
the Cardes made by the Portingales, saue those they haue
falsified of late purposely.   But nowe touching that your
Lordshippe wrote, whether that which wee discouered con-
cheth any thing the foresayde coastes: once it appeareth

New found lãd
discouered by
the englishmen.

plainely that the Newe founde lande that wee discouered is
all a mayne lande with the Indies occidentall, from whence
the emperour hath all the golde and pearles: and so continueth of coaste more then 5000. leagues of length, as by this
Carde appeareth.   For from the saide newe landes it proceedeth toward the occidēt to the Indies, and from the Indies returneth toward the orient, & after turneth southwarde
vp till it come to the straytes of Todos Sanctos, whiche I
reckon to bee more then 5000. leagues.

Note.

So that to the Indians it shoulde seeme that wee
haue some title, at least that for our discouering wee
might trade thither as other doe.   But all this is nothing
neere the spicerie.

Nowe then (if from the sayde newe founde landes the

To sayle by the
pole,

Sea bee Nauigable,) there is no doubte, but sayling
Northwarde and passing the pole descending to the equinoctiall lyne wee shall hitte these Ilandes, and it shoulde
bee muche more shorter way, then eyther the Spaniardes
or the Portingales haue.   For wee bee distaunt from the
pole but 39.degrees, and from the pole to the Equinoctiall
bee 90.the which added together bee 129.degrees, leagues
2480.and myles 7440.   Where wee shoulde finde these
Ilandes. And the Nauigation of the Spaniardes to the
spicerie is, as by this Carde you may see, from Spayne
to the Ilandes of Canarie, and from these Ilandes they
runne ouer the lyne Equinoctiall Southwarde to the cape
of the mayne lande of Indians, called the Cape of Sainte

Au-

Augustine, and from this Cape Southwardes to the
ſtraytes of Todos Sanctos, in the whiche Nauigation to
the ſayde ſtraites is 1700. or 1800. leagues : and from
theſe ſtraytes being paſt them, they returne towarde the
line Equinoctiall to the Ilandes of ſpicerie, whiche are diſtance from the ſayde ſtraites 4200 or 4300. leagues.

Or the ſtraites
of Magelan.

The Nauigation of the Portingalles to the ſayd Ilands
is, departing from Portingale Southwarde towarde the
Capo verde, and from thence to another Cape paſſing the
lyne equinoctiall called Capo de bona ſperanſa, and from
Portingale to the cape is 1800 leagues, and from this cape
to the Ilandes of ſpicerie of the Emperour is 2500.
leagues.

So that by this nauigation amounteth all to 4300 leagues.
So that as afore is ſayde , if betweene our Newe founde
landes or Norway, or Iſlande the Seas towarde the north
be Nauigable, wee ſhoulde goe to theſe Ilandes a ſhorter
way by more then 2000 leagues And though wee went not
to the ſaide Ilandes , for that they are the Emperours or
Kinges of Portingale, wee ſhoulde by the way, and comming once to the lyne Equinoctiall , finde landes no leſſe
riche of Golde and ſpicerie, as all other landes are vnder the
ſaide line Equinoctiall : and alſo ſhoulde, if wee may paſſe
vnder the North, enioye the Nauigation of all Tartarie·

Note.

Benefite to
Englande.

Which ſhould bee no leſſe profitable to our commodities
of clothe, then theſe ſpiceries to the Emperour, and king of
Portingale.

But it is a generall opinion of all Coſmographers that
paſſing the ſeuenth clyme, the ſea is all ice, the colde ſo much
that none can ſuffer it. And hitherto they had all the like opinion that vnder the lyne Equinoctiall for muche heate the
lande was inhabitable.

Obiection.

Yet ſince by experience is prooued no lande ſo much habi-
table

Anſwere.

table nor more temperate . And to conclude I thinke the ſame ſhoulde bee founde vnder the North, if it were experimented . For as all iudge, *Nihil ſit vacuum in rerum natura:* So I iudge there is no lande inhabitable, nor Sea innauigable . If I ſhould write the reaſon that preſenteth this vnto mee, I ſhoulde bee too prolixe, and it ſeemeth not requiſite for this preſent matter . God knoweth that though by it I ſhoulde haue no great intereſt, yet I haue had and ſtill haue no little minde of this buſineſſe : So that if I had facultie to my will, it ſhoulde bee þ firſt thing that I woulde vnderſtande, euen to attempt, if our Seas Northwarde bee nauigable to the Pole, or no. I reaſon, that as ſome ſickneſſes are hereditarious, & come from the father to the ſonne, ſo this inclination or deſire of this diſcouerie I inherited of my father, which with another merchant of Briſtowe named hugh Eliot were the diſcouerers of the newe found lands, of the which there is no doubt, as now plainly appeareth, if the marriners woulde then haue been ruled, and folowed their pilots mind, the lands of the weſt Indies, from whence all the gold commeth, had beene ours. For all is one coaſte, as by the carde appeareth, and is aforeſaide . Alſo in this carde by the coaſtes where you ſee C. your Lordſhip ſhall vnderſtand it is ſet for Cape or head land, where I, for Iland, where P. for Port, where R. for Riuer. Alſo in al this little carde I thinke nothing be erred touching the ſituation of the land, ſaue onely in theſe Ilands of ſpicery : which, for that as afore is ſayd, euery one ſetteth them after his minde, there can be no certification how they ſtand. I doe not denie, that there lacke many things, that a conſummate carde ſhould haue, or that a right good demonſtration deſireth . For there ſhould be expreſſed all the mountaines and riuers that are principall of name in the earth , wich the names of Portes of the ſea, the names of all principall cities , whiche all I might haue ſet, but not in this Carde, for the little ſpace would not conſent.

Your Lordſhip may ſee that ſetting only the names almoſt
of

A true opinion.

A voyage of diſcouerie by the pole.

M. Thorne and M. Eliot diſcouerers of New found land.

The cauſe why the weſt Indies were not ours: which alſo Sebaſtian Gabot writeth in a epiſtle to Baptiſt Ramuſius.

of euery region,and yet not of all, the roothe is occupied.
Many Ilands are also left out for the saide lacke of roome:
the names almost of all portes put to silence,with the roses
of the windes or pointes of the compasse : For that this is
not for Pilots to sayle by , but a summarie declaration of
that which your Lordship commaunded . And if by this
your Lordshippe cannot well perceiue the meaning of this
carde,of the which J woulde not maruell,by reason of the
rude composition of it, will it please your Lordship to aduise mee to make a bigger and a better mappe,or els that J
may cause one to bee made. For J knowe my selfe in this
and all other nothing perfect,but *Licèt semper discens,nun-
quam tamen ad perfectam scientiam peruenient.* Also J
knowe to set the forme Sphericall of the worlde in *Plano*
after the true rule of Cosmographie , it would haue been
made otherwise then this is: Howbeit the demonstration
shoulde not haue beene so plaine. And also these degrees
of longitude , that J set in the lower part of this Card,shold
haue been set along by the line cqninoctiall,and so then must
bee imagined. For the degrees of longitude neare either
of the poles are nothing equal in bignes to them in the equinoctiall. But these are set so,for that setting them a long
the Equinoctiall,it would haue made obscure a great parte
of the mappe . Many other curiosities may be required,
which for the nonce J did not set downe , as well for that
the intent J had principally was to satisfie your doubt touching the spicerie,as for that J lacke leysure and time . J
trust your Lordshippe correcting that which is erred , will
accept my good will, which is to do any thing that J maye
in your Lordshippes seruice.But from henceforth J knowe
your Lordshippe wil rather commaunde me to keepe silence,
then to be large,when you shalbe weeried with the reading
of this discourse. Jesus prosper your estate and health.

Your Lordshippes Robert
Thorne.1527.

ALſo this Carde and that which I wꝛite touching the
variaunce betweene the Emperour and the king of
Poꝛtingale, is not to bee ſhewed oꝛ communicated there
with many of that Courte . Foꝛ though there is nothing
in it pꝛeiudiciall to the Emperour, yet it may bee a cauſe of
paine to the maker : as well foꝛ that none may make theſe
Cardes, but certaine appointed and allowed foꝛ maſters, as
foꝛ that peraduenture it woulde not ſounde well to them,
that a ſtranger ſhoulde knowe oꝛ diſcouer their ſecretes: and
wolde appeare woꝛſt of all, if they vnderſtand that I wꝛite
touching ẙ ſhoꝛt way to the ſpicerie by our Seas. Though
peraduenture of troth it is not to bee looked too, as a thing
that by all opinions is vnpoſſible, and I thinke neuer
will come to effect : and therefoꝛe neither heere noꝛ els
where is it to bee ſpoken of. Foꝛ to moue it amongſt
wiſe men, it ſhoulde bee had in deriſion. And therefoꝛe
to none I woulde haue wꝛitten noꝛ ſpoken of ſuch things,
but to your Loꝛdſhip, to whome boldly I commit in this all
my fooliſh fantaſie as to my ſelfe. But if it pleaſe God
that into Englande I may come with your Loꝛdſhip, I will
ſhewe ſome coniectures of reaſon though againſt the generall opinion of Coſmographers , by which ſhall appeare this that I ſay not to lacke ſome foundation. And tyll
that time I beſeeche your Loꝛdſhip let it bee put to ſilence :
and in the meane ſeaſon it may pleaſe God to ſende our two
Engliſhmen, that are gone to the ſpicerie, which may alſo
bꝛing moꝛe plaine declaration of ẙ which in this caſe might
bee deſired. Alſo I knowe it needed not to haue beene ſo
pꝛolixe in the declaration of this Carde to your Loꝛdſhip, if
the ſaide Carde had beene very well made after the rules of
Coſmographie. Foꝛ your Loꝛdſhip woulde ſoone vnderſtande it better then I, oꝛ any other that coulde haue made
it : and ſo it ſhoulde appeare that I ſhewed *Delphinum nata-*
re. But foꝛ that I haue made it after my rude maner, it is neceſſarie that I be the declarer oꝛ gloſer of mine owne woꝛk,
oꝛ els your Loꝛdſhip ſhould haue had much labour to vnderſtande

derstande it, which nowe with it also cannot bee excused, it is so grossely done. But I knewe you looked for no curious things of mee, and therefore I trust your Lordshippe will accept this, and holde mee for excused. In other mens letters that they write they craue pardon that at this present they write no larger: but I must finish, asking pardon that at this present I write so largely. Jesus preserue your Lordship with augmentation of dignities.

Your seruant Robert Thorne. 1527.

This exhortation to king Henrie the eight, with the discourse to Doctor Ley his Ambassadour in Spaine, was preserued by one master Emmanuel Lucar executour to master Robert Thorne, and was friendly imparted vnto mee by master Cyprian Lucar his sonne an honest Gentleman and very forwarde to further any good and laudable action. And that it may bee knowne that this motion tooke present effect with the king, I thought it good herewithall to put downe the testimonie of our Chronicle that the king set out shippes for this discouerie in his life time. master Hall and master Grafton in their Chronicles write both thus: This same moneth king Henry the eight sente two faire ships, well manned and victualed, hauing in them diuers cunning men, to seeke strange regions: and so they set foorth, out of the Thames the xx. day of May in the xix. yeere of his raigne. In the yeere of our Lorde. 1527.

FINIS.

To the moſt Chriſtian king of
Fraunce, Fraunces *the firſt.*

The relation of Iohn Verarzanus a Florentine, of the
lande by him diſcouered in the name of his Maieſtie, written in *Diepe* the eight of Iuly 1524.

 Wrote not to your Maieſtie (moſt Chri-
ſtian king) ſince the time wee ſuffered
the tempeſt in the North partes, of the
ſucceſſe of the foure Ships, which your
Maieſtie ſent forth to diſcouer new lands
by the Ocean, thinking your Maieſtie
had been alreadie duly enformed thereof.
Nowe by theſe preſents I will giue your Maieſtie to vnderſtand, howe by the violence of the windes wee were forced with ye two ſhips, the Norman and the Dolphin, in ſuch
euill caſe as they were, to lande in Britaine. Whereafter
wee had repaired them in all pointes as was needefull and
armed them very well, wee tooke our courſe a long by the
coaſt of Spaine. Afterwardes with the Dolphin alone,
wee determined to make diſcouerie of newe Countries,
to proſecute the nauigation wee had alreadie begun, which
I purpoſe at this preſent to recount vnto your Maieſtie, to
make manifeſt the whole proceeding of the matter. The
17 of Ianuarie, the yeere 1524. by the grace of God, wee
departed from the diſhabited Rocke, by the Iſle of Madêra,
appertaining to the king of Portingall, with fiftie men, with
victuals, weapon, and other ſhip munition very well prouided and furniſhed for 8. monethes: And ſayling weſtwards
with a faire Eaſterly winde, in 25. dayes wee ranne 500.
leagues, and the 20. of Februarie wee were ouertaken with
as ſharpe and terrible a tempeſt as euer any ſaylers ſuffered: whereof with ye diuine helpe & mercifull aſſiſtaunce of
Almightie God, and the goodneſſe of our ſhip accompanied

A   with

with the good hap of her fortunate name, wee were deliuered, and with a prosperous wind followed our course West
& by North. And in other 25. dayes wee made aboue 400.
leagues more, where wee discouered a newe land, neuer before seene of any man either auncient or moderne, and at the
first sight it seemed somewhat lowe, but beeing within a
quarter of a league of it, wee perceiued by the great fiers
that wee sawe by the Sea coaste that it was inhabited: and
saw that the lande stretched to the Southwardes: in seeking
some conuenient harborough whereby to come a lande, and
haue knowledge of the place, wee sayled fiftie leagues in
vaine, and seeing the lande to runn still to the Southwards
wee resolued to returne backe againe towardes the North,
where we found our selues troubled with the like difficulty:
at length beeing in despaire to finde any port, wee caste
anker vpon the coast, and sent our Boate to shore, where we
sawe great store of people which came to the Sea side, and
seeing vs to approche they fled away, and sometimes would
stande still and looke backe, beholding vs with great admi-
ration: but afterwardes beeing animated and assured with
signes that wee made them, some of them came harde to the
Sea side seeming to reioyce very muche at the sight of vs,
and marueiling greatly at our apparell, shape and whitenes,
shewed vs by sundry signes where wee might most commo-
diously come a land with our Boat, offering vs also of their
victuals to eate .   Nowe I will briefly declare to your
Maiestie their life and manners, as farre as wee coulde
haue notice thereof : These people goe altogeather naked
except only that they couer their priuie partes with certaine
skinnes of beastes like vnto Marterns, which they fasten
vnto a narrowe girdle made of grasse verye artificially
wrought, hanged about with tailes of diuers other beastes,
which rounde about their bodies hang dangling downe to
their knees. Some of them weare garlandes of byrdes
feathers. The people are of colour russet , and not
much vnlike the Saracens, their hayre blacke, thicke and
not

not very long, which they tye togeather in a knot behinde
& weare it like a taile. They are wel featured in their limbs,
of meane stature and commonly somewhat bigger then we,
broode breasted, strong armes, their legges and other partes
of their bodies well fashioned, and they are disfigured in nothing sauing that they haue somewhat broode visages, and yet
not all of them: for wee sawe many of them well fauoured
hauing blacke and great eyes, with a cheerefull and stedie
looke, not strong of body yet sharpe witted, nymble and
great runners, as farre as we coulde learne by experience,
and in those two last qualities they are like to the people
of the East partes of the worlde, and especially to them of
the vttermost partes of China, wee coulde not learne of
this people their manner of liuing, nor their particuler customes by reason of ȳ short abode we made on the shore, our
companie being but small, and our ship ryding farre of in
the Sea. And not farre from these we founde an other people, whose liuing wee thinke to bee like vnto theirs, (as
heereafter I will declare vnto your Maiestie,) shewing at
this present the situation and nature of the foresaide lande:
The shore is all couered with small sande, and so ascendeth
vpwardes for the space of fifteene foote rising in forme of
little hilles about fiftie paces broade. And sayling forwards
wee founde certaine small Riuers and armes of the Sea,
that enter at certain creekes, washing the shore on both sides
as the coast lyeth. And beyonde this wee sawe the open
Countrie rising in height aboue the sandie shore with many
fayre fieldes and plaines, full of mightie great woods, some
verie thicke and some thinne, replenished with diuers sortes
of trees, as pleasaunt and delectable to beholde as is possible
to imagine. And your Maiestie may not thinke that these
are like the woodes of Hercinia or the wilde De-
sertes of Tartary, and the Northerne Coastes full
of fruitelesse trees: But full of Palme trees, Bay trees,
and high Cypresse trees, and many other sortes of trees vnknowne in Europe, which yeeld most sweete sauours farre
from the shore, the propertie whereof wee coulde not learne

for

For the cause aforesaide, and not for any difficultie to passe through the woods: Seeing they are not so thicke but that a man may passe through them. Neither doe wee thinke that they part taking of the East worlde rounde about them are all to geather voide of drugs or spicerie, and other richesse of golde, seeing the colour of the lande doth so much argue it... nd the lande is full of many beastes, as Stags, Deare and Hares, and likewise of Lakes and Pooles of Fresh water, with great plentie of foules, conuenient for all kinde of pleasant game. This lande is in latitude 34. D. with good and holsome ayre, temperate, betweene hot and colde, no vehement windes doe blowe in those Regions, and those that doe commonly raigne in those Coastes, are the North West and West windes in the Sommer season, (in the beginning whereof wee were there) the skie cleere and faire with very little raine: and if at any time the ayre bee cloudie and mistie with the Sowtherne winde immediately it is dissolued and waxeth cleare and fayre agayne. The Sea is caulme, not boysterous, the waues gentle, and although all the shore bee somewhat lowe and with out harborough: yet it is not daungerous to the saylers beeing free from rockes and deepe, so that within foure or fiue foote of the shore, there is twentie foote deepe of water without ebbe or flood, the depth still increasing in such vniforme proportion. There is very good ryding at Sea: for any Ship beeing shaken in a tempest can neuer perishe there by breaking of her cables, which wee haue proued by experince. For in the beginning of March (as is vsuall in all Regions) beeing in the Sea oppressed with Northerne windes and riding there, wee founde our anker broken before the earth sayled or mooued at all . Wee departed from this place still running a long the coaste, which we found to trende towarde the East, and wee saw euerie where verie great fiers, by reason of the multitude of the inhabitants. While we rode on that Coaste partlie because it had no harborough, and for that wee wanted water, wee sent our Boat a shore

with

Gr.34.

with 25.men: whereby reason of great and continual waues
that beate against the shore, being an open coast, without
succour, none of our men coulde possible goe a shore without
loosing our boate. We sawe there many people which came
vnto the shore, making diuers signes of friendship, and shewing that they were content wee shoulde come a lande, and by
trial we found the to be very courteous & gentle as your maiestie shal vnderstand by the successe. To the intent we might
sende them of our thinges, which the Indians commonly de-
sier and esteeme as sheetes of Paper, glasses, belles, and
such like trifles : Wee sent a young man one of our Marriners a shore, who swimming towards them, and being within 3.or 4.yeards off the shore , not trusting them, cast the
thinges vpon the shore, seeking afterwardes to returne, hee
was with such violence of the waues beaten vpon the shore,
that he was so bruised that hee lay there almost dead, whiche
the Indians perceiuing, ranne to catche him, and drawing
him out they carried him a little way off from the sea: The
young man perceiuing they caried him, beeing at the first
dismaide, began then greatly to feare and cried out pitiously,
likewise did the Indians which did accompanie him, going
about to cheere him and giue him courage, and then setting
him on the grounde at the foote of a little hill against the
sunne, beganne to beholde him with great admiration, marueiling at the whitenesse of his fleshe: And putting off his
clothes they made him warme at a great fire, not without
our great feare which remained in the boate, that they would
haue rosted him at that fire and haue eaten him. The young
man hauing recouered his strength , and hauing stayed a
while with them, shewed them by signes that hee was desirous to returne to the shippe: And they with great loue clap-
ping him fast about with many embracings, accompanying
him vnto the sea, and to put him in more assurance, leauing
him alone they went vnto a high grounde and stoode there,
beholding him vntil he was entred into the boate. This yong
man obserued as we did also, that these are of colour enclining to Blacke as the other were , with their fleshe ve-

rie

Courteous and
gentle people.

rie shining of meane stature, handsome visag, and dilicate limmes and of verie little strength:but of prompt witte, farther wee obserued not.

Departing from hence following the shore which trended somewhat towarde the North in 50.leagues space, wee came to another lande which shewed much more faire and full of woods,being very great, where we rode at Ancker, and that wee might haue some knowledge thereof, wee sent 20.men a lande, which entred into the countrey about two leagues,and they founde that the people were fledde to the woods for feare, they sawe onely one olde woman with a young maide of 18.or 20.yeeres olde,which seeing our companie hid them selues in the grasse for feare,the olde woman caried two Infantes on her shoulders,and behinde her necke a childe of 8.yeeres olde : the yong woman was laden likewise with as many:but when our men came vnto them, the women cryed out,the olde woman made signes that the men were fled vnto the woods, as soone as they sawe vs to quiet them and to winne their fauour, our men gaue them suche victuals as they had with them to eate,which the old woman receiued thankfully:but the yong woman disdained them al, and threwe them disdainefully on the grounde, they tooke a childe from the olde woman to bring into Fraunce, and going about to take the young woman which was verye beautifull & of tal stature, they could not possibly for ye great outcries that shee made bring her to the sea, and especially hauing great woods to passe through, and being farre from the shippe,wee purposed to leaue her behinde bearing away the childe onely. We found those folkes to bee more white than those that we founde before, being clad with certaine leaues ye hang on boughes of trees, which they sowe together with thredes of wilde hempe, their heads were trussed vp after the same manner as the former were, their ordinarie foode is of pulse,whereof they haue great store, differing in colour & taste from ours,of good & plasant taste. Moreouer they liue by fishing & fouling which they take with ginnes, and bowes made of hard wood the arrowes of Canes,being

hea-

headed with the bones of fishe and other beastes. The beastes in these partes are much wilder thē in our Europe, by reason they are continually chased and hunted. Wee sawe many of their boates made of one tree 20. foote long, and 4. foote broade, which are not made with Iron, or stone, or any other kinde of metal, (because that in all this countrie for the space of 200. leagues whiche we ranne, wee neuer sawe one stone of any sort): they help themselues with fyre, burning so much of the tree as is sufficient for the hollownesse of the boate, the like they doe in making the sterne and the foreparte vntill it be fitte to saile vpon the sea. The lande is in situation, goodnesse and fairenes like the other: it hath woods like the other, thinne and full of diuers sortes of trees: but not so sweete because the countrey is more northerly and cold.

Wee sawe in this Countrey many Uines growing naturally, which growing vp take hold of the trees as they do in Lombardie, tō if by husbandmen they were dressed in good order, without all doubte they woulde yeelde excellent wines: for wee hauing oftentymes seene the fruite thereof dried, whiche was sweete and pleasaunt, and not differing from ours. Wee doe thinke that they doe esteeme the same, because that in euery place where they growe, they take away the vnder braunches growing rounde about, that the fruite thereof may ripen the better.

We found also roses, violettes, lillies, and many sorts of herbes, and sweete and odoriferous flowers different from ours. We knewe not their dwellinges, because they were farre vp in the lande, and wee iudge by manye signes that wee sawe, that they are of wood and of trees framed together.

Wee doe beleeue also by many coniectures and signes, that many of them sleeping in the fieldes, haue no other couer then the open skye. Further knowledge haue wee not of them, we thinke ŷ all the rest whose countreys we passed liue all after one manner, hauing our aboade three dayes in this cuntrey, riding on the coast for want of harborougbs,

A 4

concluded to departe from thence, trending along the shore betweene the North and the East, sayling onely in the day-time, & riding at ancker by night in the space of 100.leagues sayling, wee founde a very pleasant place, situated amongst certaine litle steepe hilles : from amiddest the which hilles there ran down into the sea a great streame of water, which within the mouth was very deep,& from ÿ sea to ÿ mouth of same with the tyde which wee found to rise 8.foot,any great vessell laden may passe vp.

But because wee rode at Ancker in a place well fensed from the winde,wee woulde not venture our selues without knowledge of the place, and wee passed vp with our boate onely into the sayde Riuer, and sawe the Countrey very wel peopled.The people are almost like vnto the others,and clad with the fethers of foules of diuers colours, they came to-wardes vs very cherefully, making great showtes of admi-ration,shewing vs where we might come to lande most safe-ly with our boate.We entred vp the said riuer into the lande about halfe a league, where it made a most pleasant lake a-bout 3.leagues in compasse: on the which they rowed from the one side to the other to the number of 30. of their small boates:wherein were many people whiche passed from one shore to the other to come and see vs, and beholde vpon the sodaine(as it is wont to fall out in sayling)a contrarie flawe of winde comming from the sea, wee were enforced to re-turne to our Shippe, leauing this lande to our great dis-contentment, for the great commoditie and pleasantnesse

The pleasant-nes and riches of the lande.

thereof whiche wee suppose is not without some ri-ches,all the hills shewing minerall matters in thē.We wet-ed Ancker,and sayled towarde the East, for so the coast tren-ded,and so alwayes for 50. leagues being in the sight ther e-

The descriptiō of Claudia I-lande.

of wee discouered an Ilande in forme of a triangle, dis-tant from the maine lande 3.leagues, about the bignesse of the Ilande of the Rodes, it was full of hilles couered with trees,well peopled, for we sawe fires all along the coaste,

Claudia was wife of King Francis.

wee gaue the name of it,of your Maiesties mother, not stay-ing there by reason of the weather being contrarie.

And

And wee came to another lande being 15. leagues distant from the Ilande, where wee founde a passing good hauen, wherein being entred we founde about 20. small boates of the people which with diuers cries and wondrings came about our shippe, comming no nerer then 50. paces towards vs, they stayed and behelde the artificialnesse of our ship, our shape & apparel, thã they al made a loud showte together declaring that they reioyced: when we had something animated them vsing their geastes, they came so neere vs that wee cast them certaine bells and glasses and many toyes, whiche when they had receiued they lookte on them with laughing & came without feare aborde our ship. There were amongst these people 2, kings of so goodly stature and shape as is possible to declare, the eldest was about 40. yeeres of ag, the second was a yong man of 20. yeres old. Their apparell was on this maner, the elder had vpõ his naked body a harts skin wrought artificialie with diuers braunches like Damaske, his head was bare with the haire tyed vp behinde with diuers knottes: About his necke he had a large chaine, garnished with diuers stones of sundrie colours the young man was almost appareled after the same manner. This is the goodliest people and of the fairest conditions that wee haue found in this our voyage. They exceed vs in bignes, they are of the colour of brasse, some of thẽ encline more to whitnes: others are of yellowe colour, of comely visage with long & blacke heire which they are very carefull to trim and decke vp, they are blacke and quicke eyed. I write not to your Maiestie, of the other parte of their bodie, hauing all suche proportion as appertayneth to anye handsome man.   The women are of the like conformitie and Beawtie, verie handsome and well fauoured, they are as well mannered and continente as anye women, of good education, they are all naked saue their priuie partes whiche they couer with a Deares skinne braunched or embrodered as the men vse: there are also of them whiche weare on their armes verie riche skinnes of leopardes, they adorne their heades with diuers ornamentes made of their owne heire, whiche hange

The Countr of Sir H. G. voyage.

B   downe

downe before or both sides their brestes, others vse other kinde of dressing them selues like vnto the women of Egypt and Syria, these are of the elder sorte: and when they are married they weare diuers toyes, according to the vsage of the people of the East as well men as women.

Among whom wee sawe many plates of wrought coper, which they esteeme more then golde, whiche for the colour they make no accompt of, for that among all other it is counted the basest, they make most accompt of Azure and red. The things that they esteemed most of al those which we gaue them were bels, cristall of Azure colour, and other toies to hang at their eares or about their necke. They did not desire cloth of silke or of golde, muche lesse of any other sorte, neither cared they for thinges made of steele and Iron, which wee often shewed them in our armour whiche they made no wonder at, and in beholding them they onely asked the arte of making them: the like they did at our glasses, which whē the behelde, they sodainely laught and gaue them vs againe. They are very liberal for they giue that which they haue, we became great friendes with these, and one day wee entred into the hauen with our shippe, where as before wee rode a league of at sea by reason of the contrary weather. They came in great companies of their small boates vnto the ship with their faces all be painted with diuers colours, shewing vs ý it was a signe of ioy, bringing vs of their victuals, they made signes vnto vs where wee might safest ride in the hauen for the safegarde of our shippe keeping still our companie: and after we were come to an Ancker, we bestowed fifteene dayes in prouiding our selues many necessary things, whether euery day the people repayred to see our ship bringing their wiues with them, whereof they are very ielous: and they themselues entring abrode the shippe and stayinge there a good space, caused their wiues to stay in their boates, and for al the intreatie we could make, offering to giue them diuers things, we could neuer obtaine that they would suffer them to come aborde our ship. And oftentimes one of the two kings comming with his queene, and many gentlemen for their pleasure to see vs, they all stayed on ý shore two hundred paces fró vs, sending a smal boate to giue vs intelligéce of their comming, saying they would come to see our shippe, this they did in token of safetye, and assoone as they had answere from vs they came immediatly, and hauing stayed a while to beholde it, they wondered at hearing the cryes and noyes of the marriners. The queene and her maids stayed in a very light boate, at an Iland a quarter of a leage off, while the king abode a long space in our ship vttering diuers conceites with geastures, biewing with great admiration, all the furniture of the shippe, demaunding the propertie of euerie thing perticularly. He tooke likewise great pleasure in beholding our apparell, and in tasting our meates, and so courteously taking his leaue departed. And sometimes our men staying for two or three dayes on a litle Ilande nere the ship for diuers necessaries, (as it is ý vse of seamen) he returned with 7. or 8. of his gentlemen to see what we did, and asked of vs oft times if wee meant to make any long aboade there, offering vs of their prouision: then the king drawing his bowe and running vp and downe with his gentlemen, made much sporte to gratifie our men, wee were oftentimes within the lande 5. or 6. leagues, which we found as pleasant as is possible to declare very apt for any kinde of husbandry of corne, wine and oyle: for that there are plaines 25. or 30. leagues broad, open and without any impediment of trees of such fruitfulnesse, that any seede being sowne therein, will bring forth most excellent fruite. We entred afterwards into the woods which wee found so great and thicke, that any armie were it neuer so great might haue hid it selfe therein, the trees whereof are okes, cipres trees, and other sortes vnknowen in Europe. We found Pomi appii, Damson trees, and Nutte trees, and many other sorts of fruits differing fró ours: there are beasts in great abundance, as hartes, deares, leopardes, and other kinds which they take with their nets & bowes which are their chiefe weapons, the arrowes whiche they vse are made with great cunning, and in steade of iron, they head them with smeriglio, wt iasper stone, & hard marble & other sharp stones which they vse in stead of iron to cut

trees,

trees,and make their boates of one whole piece of wood,ma-
king it hollowe with great and wonderfull art,wherein 10.
oꝛ 12. men may bee cōmodiouſly, their oares are ſhoꝛte and
bꝛoad at the ende, and they vſe them in the ſea without anye
daunger,and by maine foꝛce of armes,with as great ſpeedi-
neſſe as they liſte them ſelues. We ſawe their houſes made
in circuler oꝛ rounde fourme 10. oꝛ 12. foote in compaſſe,
made with halfe circles of timber, ſeperate one from another without any oꝛder of building, couered with mattes of
ſtrawe wꝛought cunningly together, which ſaue them from
the winde and raine,and if they had the oꝛder of building and
perfect ſkil of woꝛkmāſhip as we haue:there were no doubt
but ꝑ they would alſo make eftſoones great and ſtately buildings. Foꝛ all the ſea coaſtes are full of cleare and gliſtering
ſtones,and alablaſter, and therefoꝛe it is full of good hauens
and harbarours foꝛ ſhips. They mooue the foꝛeſaide houſes
from one place to another accoꝛding to the commoditie of
the place and ſeaſon wherein they will make their aboade,
and only taking of the couer,they haue other houſes builded
incontinent. The father and the whole familie dwell together in one houſe in great number : in ſome of them we ſawe
25.oꝛ 30. perſons.They feede as the other doe afoꝛeſaide of
pulſe whiche doe growe in that countrey with better oꝛder
of huſbandꝛy thē in the others.They obſerue in their ſowing
the courſe of the Moone and the riſing of certaine ſtarres,
and diuers other cuſtomes ſpoken of by antiquitie. Moꝛeo-
uer,they liue by hunting and fiſhing. they liue long,and are
ſeldome ſicke , and if they chaunce to fall ſicke at any time,
they heale them ſelues with fire without any phiſition, and
they ſay that they die foꝛ very age.They are very pitiful and
charitable towardes their neighbours, they make great la-
mentations in their aduerſitie ⁊ in their miſerie,the kinred
recken vp all their felicitie,at their departure out of life,they
vſe mourning mixt w̄ ſinging, w̄ continueth foꝛ a lōg ſpace.
This is aſmuch as wee coulde learne of them.This lande is
ſituated in the Paralele of Rome,in 41.degrees ⁊2.terces:
but

but somewhat more colde by accidentall cause and not of nature,(as I will declare vnto your highnesse els where) describing at this present the situation of the foresaide countrie, which lyeth East and West, I say that the mouth of the hauen lyeth open to the South halfe a league broade, and being entred within it betweene the East and the North, it stretcheth twelue leagues: where it waxeth broder and broder, and maketh a gulfe aboute 20. leagues in compasse, wherein are fiue small Islandes very fruitfull and pleasant, full of hie and broade trees,among the which Ilandes, any great Nauie may ryde safe without any feare of tempest or other daunger. Afterwardes turning towards the South and in the entring into the Hauen on both sides there are most pleasant hilles, with many riuers of most cleere water falling into the Sea.

In the middest of this entraunce there is a rock of free stone growing by nature apt to builde any Castle or Fortresse there,for y keeping of the hauen.The fift of May being furnished with all thinges necessarie,we departed from y said Coast keeping along in the sight thereof,& we sayled 150 leagues finding it all wayes after one manner: but the lande somewhat higher with certaine mountaines all which beare a shewe of minerall matter, wee sought not to lande there in any place,because the weather serued our turne for sayling: but wee suppose that it was like to the former, the Coast ranne Eastward for the space of fiftie leagues. And trending afterwardes the North, wee founde another lande high full of thicke woods,the trees whereof were firres,Cipresses and such like as are wont to growe in colde Countries. The people differ much from the other,& looke how much the former seemed to be courteous and gentle:so much were these full of rudenesse and ill manners, and so barbarous that by no signes that euer wee coulde make,wee could haue any kinde of trafficke with them. They cloth theselues with Beares skinnes and Leopardes and sealles and other beastes skinnes. Their foode as farre as wee coulde per-

cieue,

ceiue, repayring often vnto their dwellings wee fuppofe to bee by hunting and fifhing, and of certaine fruites, which are a kinde of rootes, which the earth yeeldeth of her owne accord. They haue no graine, neither fawe wee any kinde or figne of tyllage, neither is the lande, for the barrennes thereof apt to beare frute or feed. If at any time we defired by exchaunge to haue any of their commodities, they vfed to come to the Sea fhore vpon certaine craggie rocks, and wee ftanding in our Boats, they let downe with a rope what it pleafed them to giue vs, crying continually that wee fhould not approch to the lande, demanding immediately the exchange taking nothing but kniues, fifhookes and tooles to cut withall, neither did they make any account of our curtefie. And when we had nothing left to exchange with them, when we departed from them the people fhewed all fignes of difcourtefie and difdaine, as was poffible for any creature to inuent. Wee were in defpight of them two or three leagues within the lande, being in number 25. armed men of vs: And when wee went on fhore they fhot at vs with their bowes, making great outcries, and afterwardes fled into the woods. Wee founde not in this lande any thing notable, or of importance, fauing very great woods and certaine hilles, they may haue fome mynerall matter in them, becaufe wee fawe many of thē haue beadftones of Copper hanging at their eares. We departed from thence keeping our courfe North Eaft along the coafte, which wee founde more pleafant champion and without woods, with high mountaines within the lande continuing directly along the coaft for the fpace of fiftie leagues, wee difcouered 32. Ilelandes lying all neare the lande, being fmall and pleafant to the biewe, high and hauing many turnings and windings betwene them, making many fayre harboroughes and chanels as they doe in the goulfe of Venice in Saluonia, and Dalmatia, wee had no knowledge or acquaintance with the people: wee fuppofe they are of the fame maners and nature that the others are. Sayling Northeaft for the fpace of 150. leagues we approched

ched to the lande that in times past was discouered by the Britons, which is in fiftie degrees. Hauing now spent all our prouision and victuals, and hauing discouered about 700. leagues and more of newe Countries, and being furnished with Water and Wood wee concluded to returne into Fraunce.

Touching the religion of this people, which wee haue founde for want of their language we could not vnderstand neither by signes nor gesture that they had any religion or lawe at all, or that they did acknowledge any first cause or mouer, neither that they worship the heauen or starres the Sunne or Moone or other Planets, and much lesse whether they bee idolaters, neither coulde wee learne whether that they vsed any kinde of Sacrifices or other adorations, neither in their villages haue they any Temples or houses of prayer. We suppose that they haue no religion at all, and ȳ they liue at their owne libertie. And ȳ all this proceedeth of ignorance, for that they are very easie to bee persuaded: and all that they see vs Christians doe in our diuine seruice they did the same with the like imitation as they sawe vs to doe it.

B 4   The

❧ The difcouerie of the Ifles of Frif-
land, Iſeland, Engroueland, Eſtotiland, Drogeo and
Icaria, made by M. Nicolas Zeno, Knight, and M. An-
tonio his brother.

In the yere of our Lord 1200. There was in the Citie of Venice a famous Gentleman, named M. Marino Zeno, who for his great vertue and singular wisedome, was called and elected gouernour in certain common wealthes of Italy, in the administration whereof hee bore himselfe so discreetly, that hee was beloued of all men, and his name greatly reuerenced of those that neuer knewe or sawe his person. And among sundrie his worthie workes, this is recorded of him, that hee pacified certaine greeuous ciuile dissentions that arose among the Cittzens of Verona: whereas otherwise if by his graue aduise and great diligence, they had not beene preuented, the matter was likely to breake out in hot broiles

Podeſta.

of warre. Hee was the first Agent that the common wealth of Venice kept in Conſtantinople in the yeere 1205. *quando n'era patrona, conli baroni frãcesi.* This Gentleman had a sonne named M. Pietro, who was the father of the Duke Rinieri, which Duke dying with out issue, made his heyre M. Andrea, the sonne af M. Marco his brother. This M. Andrea was captaine generall and Procurator, a man of great reputation for many rare partes, that were in him. He had a sonne M. Rinieri, a worthie Senatour and prudent Councellour: Of whom descende M. Pietro Generall of the league of the Chriſtians againſt the Turkes, who was called Dragon, for that in his armes hee bare a Dragon. Hee was father to M. Carlo the famous Procurator and Generall againſte the Genowayes in
thoſe

those cruel warres, when as almost all the chiefe princes of Europe did oppugne and seek to ouerthrow our Empire and libertie, where by his great valiancie and prowesse like an other Furius Camillus, he deliuered his Countrie from the present perill it was in, being readie to become a pray & spoyle vnto the enemie, wherefore hee was afterwarde surnamed, the Lion, and for an eternall remembrance of his fortitude and valiant exploits he gaue the Lion in his armes. M. Carlo had two brethren, M. Nicolo, the knight & Antonio, the father M. Dragon, of whom issued M. Caterino, the father of M. Pietro, this M. Pietro had sonnes M. Caterino, that dyed the last yeere, M. Francisco, M. Carlo, M. Battista, and M. Vincenzo. That M. Caterino was father to M. Nicolo, that is yet liuing. Now M. Nicolo, the knight, being a man of great courage and very nobly minded, after this foresaide warre of Genoua, that troubled so our predecessours, entred into a wonderfull great desire and fansie to see the fashions of the world, and to trauaile, and to acquaint himselfe with the manners of sundry nations & learne their languages, wherby afterwards vpon occasions hee might be y better able to do seruice to his coūtrie & purchase to himselfe credite & honor. Wherfore hee caused a shippe to bee made & hauing furnished her at his proper charges (as hee was very wealthie) hee departed out of our Seas & passing the straites of Gibralterra, he sailed for certaine dayes vpon y Ocean keeping his course stil to y Northwards, w intent to see England and Flaunders. Where being assaulted in those Seas by a terrible tempest, was so tossed for the space of many dayes with the Sea and winde that hee knewe not where hee was, till at length hee discouered lande, and not beeing able any longer to sustaine the violence of the tempest the ship was cast away vpon the Isle of Friseland. The men were saued, and most part of the goods that were in the Ship. And this was in the yeere 1380. The inhabitants of the Iland came running in great multitudes w weapons to set vpon M. Nicolo and his men, who beeing sore wether beaten and ouerlaboured at Sea, and not knowing in what

The ship of M. N. Zeno cast away vpon Friseland in anno. 1380.

C   pars

part of the wozlde they were, were not able to make any rc-
fiftaunce at all, much leffe to defende them felues couragi-
oufly, as it behooued them in fuch dangerous cafe. And
they fhoulde haue beene doubteleffe very difcourteoufly en-
treated and cruelly handeled, if by good hap there had not
been hard by the place a Pzince with armed people. Who
bnderftanding, that there was euen at that pzefent a great
fhip caft away vpon the Jland, came running at the noyfe
and outcries that they made againft our poze Mariners,

A fozraine
pzince hapning
to be in Frifläd
w armed men.
When M. Zeno
fuffered fhip-
wzack, there
came vnto him
and fpake latin.

and dziuing away the inhabitants, fpake in latine and afked
them what they were and from whence they came, and perceiuing y they were Jtalians, z all of one Countrie, he was
furpzifed with marueilous great ioy. Wherefoze pzomi-
fing theall, that they fhoulde receiue no difcourtefie, and that
they were come into a place where they fhoulde bee well v-
fed and very welcome, he tooke them into his pzotection vpon his faith. This was a great Lozd and poffeffed certaine
Jlands called Porland, lying one the Southfide of Frifland
being y richeft and moft populous of all thofe partes, his

Zichmni pzince
of Pozland oz
Duke of Sozani.

name was Zichmni: z befide the faid little Jlands, he was
Duke of Sorani, lying within the land towards Scotland.
Of thefe Nozth partes I thought good to dzaw the copie of
a Sea carde, which amongeft other antiquities, J haue in
my houfe, which although it be rotten thzough many yeres:
yet it falleth out indifferent well, and to thofe that are de-
lighted in thefe things, it may ferue foz fome light to the vnderftanding of that, which without it cannot fo eafily be con-
ceiued. Zichmni being Lozde of thofe Seignozies (as is
faid) was a very warlike and valiant man z aboue al things
famous in Sea caufes. And hauing this yeere befoze gi-

Frifland the
king of Noz-
wayes.

uen the ouerthzowe to the king of Norway, who was Lozd
of the Jlande, beeing defirous to winne fame by feates of
armes, was come on land with his mē to giue the attēpt, foz
y winning of Frifland, which is an Jland much bigger then
Jreland. Wherefoze feeing that M. Nicolo was a mā of
iudgement and difcretion, and very expert beth in Sea matters and martiall affaires, hee gaue him commiffion to goe
abozd his nauie with all his men, charging the captaine to

honour him and in all things to vse his counsaile. This Nauie of Zichmni was of thirteene vessels, wherof two only were with oares, the rest small barkes, and one ship, with the which they sayled to the Westwardes and with little paines wonne Ledouo and Ilofe and diuers other small Ilandes, and turning into a bay called Sudero, in the hauen of the towne named Sanestol they tooke certaine small Barks laden with salt fish. And heere they founde Zichmni, who came by land with his armie conquering all the countrie as he went, they staied here but a while but held on their course to the Westwards till they came to the other Cape of the goulfe or bay, then turning againe they found certaine Ilelandes and broken landes which they reduced all vnto the Seignorie and possession of Zichmni. These Seas for as much as they sayled, were in maner nothing but sholds and rocks, in sort that if M. Nicolo and the venetian mariners had not beene their Pilots, the whole Fleete in iudgement of all that were in it, had been cast away, so small was ye skill of Zichmnis men in respect of ours, who had been trained vp in the art and practise of nauigation all the daies of their life. Now the Fleete hauing doone such things, (as is declared) ye Captaine by the counsel of M. Nicolo, determined to goe a lande at a towne called Bondendon, to vnderstande what successe Zichmni had in his warres, where they heard to their great content, that he had fought a great battaile and put to flight the armie of his enemie: by reason of which victorie they sent Embassadours from all partes of the Ilande to yeeld, the countrie vp into his handes, taking down their enseignes in euery towne and castell: They thought good to stay in that place for his comming, being reported for certaine that he would bee there very shortly. At his comming there was great congratulatiõ and many signes of gladnes shewed, as wel for the victorie by lande as for that by Sea, for the which the venetians were honoured & extolled of all men, in such sort ye there was no talke but of them, and of ye great valour of M. Nicolo. Wherfore the Prince who was a great fauourer of valiant men and especially of those that

coulde

coulo behaue them felues well at the Sea, caufeo M. Nicolo to bee brought before him, and after hauing commended
him with many honourable fpeeches, and prayfed his great
induftrie and dexterie of wit, by the which, he acknowledged
himfelfe to haue receiued an ineftimable benefite as the fauing of his Fleete and the winning of many places, he made

M. Zeno, made knight by Zichmni.

him Knight, and rewarded his men with many riche and
bountifull giftes : Then departing from thence they went
in triumphing maner towardes Frifeland, the chief Citie of

*Ships laden with fifh at frif-
land: for Flaun-
ders, Britaine,
England, Scot-
land, Norway,
and Denmark.*

ye Ilande, fituate on the Southeft fide of the Ifle, within a
goulf, (as there are very many in that Iland). In this goulfe
or bay there is fuch great abundance of fifh taken, that many
ships are laden therewith to ferue Flaunders, Britaine, England, Scotland, Norway and Denmarke, and by this trade
they gather great wealth.

*But not to bee
proued that euer
any came theece.
A letter fent by
mafter M. Zeno
from Frifeland
to his brother,
M. Antonio in
Uenice.
End of the firft
letter.*

And thus much is taken out of a letter, that M. Nicolo
fent vnto M. Antonio his brother, requefting him that hee
woulde feeke fome meanes to come to him.   Wherefore
hee, who had as great defire to trauaile as his brother,
bought a Ship, and directing his courfe that way, after hee
had fayled a great while and efcaped many dangers, hee arriued at length in fafetie with M. Nicolo, who receiued him
very ioyfully, for that hee was his brother not only in flefhe
and blood, but alfo in valour and good qualities .   M. Antonio remained in Frifelande and dwelt there for the fpace
of fourteene yeeres, foure yeeres with M. Nicolo, and ten
yeeres alone.   Where they came into fuch grace and fauour with the Prince, that hee made M. Nicolo, Captaine
of his Nauie, & with great preparation of warre they were
fent foorth for the enterprife of Eftlande, which lyeth vpon
the coafte betweene Frifeland and Norway, where they did
many domages, but hearing that the king of Norway was
comming towardes them with a great Fleet, they departed
w fuch a terrible flaw of wind ye they were driue vpo certaine
fholdes. Where a great part of their ships were caft away, ye
reft were faued vpo Grifland, a great Iland but difhabited.

The

The king of Norway his fleete being taken with the same storme, did vtterly perishe in those seas. Whereof Zichmni hauing notice, by a shippe of his enemies, that was cast by chaunce vpon Grisland. Hauing repayred his fleete, and perceyuing him selfe northerly neere vnto the Islandes, determined to set vpon Islande, which together with the rest was subiect to the king of Norway: But he founde the countrey so well fortified and defended, that his fleete beeing so small and very ill appointed both of weapons and men, hee was gladde to retire. And so hee left that enterprise without perfourming any thing at all, and in the same chanelles he assaulted þ other Iles called the Islands, which are seuen Talas, Broas, Iscant, Trans, Mimant, Dambere, & Bres, and hauing spoyled them all, hee built a fort in Bres, where he left M.Nicolo, with certaine small barkes and men and munition. And nowe thinking he had done well for this voyage, with those fewe shippes which were left hee returned into Frieslande. M.Nicolo remayning nowe in Bres determined vpon a time to goe forth and discouer lande, wherefore arming out their small barkes in the moneth of Iuly, he sayled to the Northwardes, and arriued in Engrouelande. Where he founde a monastery of Fryers of the order of the Predicators, and a Church dedicated to S. Thomas harde by a hill, that casteth forth fire, like Vesuuius and Etna.

Engrouelande. Preaching Friers of S. Thomas.

There is a fountayne of hot burning water with the whiche they heate the Churche of the monasterie and the Fryers chambers, it commeth also into the kitchen so boyling hotte, that they vse no other fire to dresse their meate, and putting their bread into brasse pottes without any water, it doeth bake as it were in a hot ouen. They haue also small gardens, couered ouer in the winter time, which being watered with this water are defended from the force of the snowe and colde, which in those parts being situate farre vnder the pole, is very extreeme; and by this meanes they produce flowers and fruites and herbes of sundrie sortes, euen as in other temperate countreys in their seasons in suche sorte that the rude and sauage people of those partes seeing these su-

A notable

pernaturall

pernaturall effectes doe take those Friers for Gods, and bring them many presentes as chickens, flesh and diuers other thinges,and haue them all in great reuerence as Lords. When the frost and snowe is great, they heate their houses in maner before said,and will by letting in the water or opening the windowes,temper the heate and colde at their pleasure. In y buildings of the monastery they vse no other matter but that which is ministred vnto them by the fire,for they take the burning stones,that are cast out as it were sparkles or ceindres at the firie mouth of the hill, and when they are most enflamed,cast water vpon them,wherby they are dissolued and become excellēt white lime and so tough that being contriued in building it lasteth for euer. And the very sparkles after the fire is out of them do serue in steede of stones to make walles and vautes: for being once colde they will neuer dissolue or breake except they be cut with some irō toole, and the vautes that are made of them are so light that they need no suftentacle or proppe to holde them vp,and they wil endure continually very fayre and whole. By reason of these great commodities the friers haue made there so many buildings and walles,that it is a wonder to see. The couerts or roofes of their houses for the most part are made in this maner,first they rayse the wall vp to his full height, then they make it enclining or bowing in by litle and litle in forme of a vaute. But they are not greatly troubled with raine in those partes,for that, by reason of the pole or colde climate, the first snowe being falne it thaweth no more for the space of nine moneths,for so long dureth their winter. They feede of the fleshe of wilde beastes & of fish,for where as the warme water falleth into the sea, there is a large and wide hauen, which by reason of the heate of the water, doeth neuer freeze all the winter, by meanes whereof there is suche concourse and flocks of sea foule and such aboundance of fishe,that they take thereof infinite multitudes, whereby they maintayne a great number of people rounde about whiche they keepe in continuale worke,both in building and taking of foules and fishe,and in a thousande other necessarie affaires and busines

about

about the monafterie.

Their houfes are builte about the hill on euery fide, in fourme rounde, and 25. foote broade, and in mounting vpwardes they goe narower and narower, leauing at the toppe a litle hole, whereat the ayre commeth in, to giue light to the houfe, and the flore of the houfe is fo hot, that being within they feele no colde at all. Hither in the fommer time come many barkes from the Ilands there about, & from the Cape aboue Norway and from Trondon. And bring to the Friers al maner things that may be defired, taking in change thereof fifhe which they drie in the funne or in the colde, and fkins of diuers kindes of beaftes. For the which they haue wood to burne and timber verie artificially carued, and corne & cloth to make them apparell. For in change of the two forefayde commodities all the nations bordering rounde about them couet to trafficke with them, and fo they without any trauell or expences haue that which they defire. To this monafterie reforte Friers of Norway, of Suetia and of other countreys but the moft part are of the Iflandes. There are continually in that part many barkes, whiche are kept in there by reafon of the fea being frozen, wayting for the feafon of the yeere to diffolue the Ice. The fifhers boates are made like vnto a weners fhuttle, taking the fkins of fifhes, they fafhió them with the bones of the fame fifhes, and fowing thé together in many doubles they make them fo fure and fubftanciall, that it is miraculous to fee, how in tempefts they will fhut théfelues clofe within, and let the fea and winde carrie them, they care not whether, without any feare eyther of breaking or drowning. And if they chance to be driuen vpõ any rocks, they remaine founde, without the leaft brufe in the worlde: And they haue as it were a fleeue in the bottome which is tied faft in ý middle, & when there cõmeth any water into their boat, they put it into the one halfe of ý fleeue, thé faftning ý ende of it ñ two peeces of wood and loofing ý band beneath they conuey the water forth of the boate: and this they doe as often as they haue occafion without any perill or impediment at all. Moreouer, the water of the monafterie being of fulphurious

Trade in fommer time from Trondon to S. Thomas friers in Ingrouclãd.

Refort of friers from Norway & Sueden, to the monafterie in Ingrouelande called S. Thf.

C 4

ſ brimſtone nature is conueyed into the lodginges of the
principall Friers by certaine veſſels of braſſe, tinne or ſtone
ſo hotte that it heateth the place as it were a ſtowe, not carry-
ing with it any ſtinke or other noyſome ſmell.

Beſides this they haue another conueyance to bring
hot water with a wall vnder the ground to the ende it ſhould
not freeſe, vnto the middle of the court, where it falleth into a great veſſel of braſſe, that ſtandeth in the middle of a boyling fountayne, and this is to heate their water to drinke and
to water their gardens, and thus they haue from the hill the
greateſt commodities that may be wiſhed, and ſo theſe Fryers employ all their trauaile and ſtudie for the moſt part in
trimming their gardins and in making faire and beawtifull
buildings and eſpecially handſome and commodious, neyther are they deſtitute of ingenious and painefull artificers
for the purpoſe, for they giue very large payment, and to
them that bring them fruites and ſeedes they are very bountifull and giue they care not what. So that there is great
reſort of workemen and maiſters in diuers faculties, by reaſon of the good gaines and large allowance that is there.

The moſt of them ſpeake the Latin tongue, and eſpecially
the ſuperiours and principalls of the monaſterie. And this
is as muche as is knowen of Engrouelande, which is all by
the relation of M. Nicolo, who maketh alſo particular de-
ſcription of a riuer, that he diſcouered, as is to be ſeene in
the carde that I drewe. And in the ende M. Nicolo not being vſed and acquainted with theſe cruell coldes, fell ſicke,
and a litle while after returned into Friſlande, where he dyed. He left behinde him in Venice two ſonnes, M. Giouanni
and M. Toma, who had two ſonnes M. Nicolo, the father of
the famous Cardinal Zeno, and M. Pietro of whom deſcen-
ded the other Zenos, that are liuing at this day.

Now M. Nicolo being dead, M. Aotonio ſucceeded him both
in his goods and in his dignities & honour, and albeit he attempted diuers wayes and made greate ſupplication hee
coulde neuer obtaine licence to returne into his Countrey.
For Zichmni had determined to make him ſelfe Lorde of
the

In the monaſta-
rie S. Thomas
moſt of them
ſpeake the latin
tongue.
and of the two
letter.

M. Zeno died in
Friſlande.

the sea. Wherefore vsing alwayes the counsaile and ser=
uice of M. Antonio, hee sent hym with some small barkes
to the Westwardes, for that towardes those partes some of
his fishermen had discouered certaine Ilandes verye rich
and populous, whiche discouerie, M. Antonio in a letter
to his brother M. Carlo, recounteth from point to point in
this manner, sauing that wee haue chaunged some olde
woordes, leauing the matter entire as it was

Sixe and twentie yeeres agoe there departed foure
Fisher boates, the whiche a mightie tempest arising, were
tossed for the space of manye dayes verye desperately vpon
the Sea, when at length the tempeste ceassyng and the
weather waxing fayre they discouered an Ilande called Es=
cotilande, lying to the Westwardes aboue 1000. Miles
from Frislande, vpon the whiche one of the boates was
caste awaye, and sixe men that were in it were taken of the
inhabitauntes and brought vnto a verye fayre and populous
Citie, where the kyng of the place sent for manye in=
terpreters, but there was none coulde bee founde that vn=
derstoode the language of the fishermen, excepte one that
spake Latin, who was also cast by chaunce vpon the same I=
lande, who in the behalfe of the kyng asked them what
Countreymen they were, and so vnderstanding theyr
case, rehearsed it vnto the King, who willed that they
shoulde tarrie in the Countrey, wherefore they obeyinge
his commaundement for that they coulde not otherwise doe,
dwelte fiue yeeres in the Ilande, and learned the lan=
guage, and one of them was in diuers partes of the Ilande,
and reporteth that it is a verye riche Countrey, abounding
with all the commodities of the worlde, and that it is little
lesse than Islande, but farre more fruitefull, hauing in
the middle thereof a verye hyghe mountayne, from the
whiche there riseth foure Riuers, that passe throughe the
whole Countrey.

The inhabitantes are very wittie people, and haue all
the artes and faculties as wee haue: and it is credible, that
in time past they haue had trafficke with our men, for he

3. letter begin-
neth from the
second brother
M. Antonio out
of Frislande, to
his other bro-
ther in Venice
named Mester
Carlo.
Escotiland.
6. fisher men
taken.

Fishermen of
Frislande spake
latin.

Sixe were 5.
yeeres in Esco-
tilande.

One of the fish-
ers of Frisland
reporteth of Es-
cotilande.
Escotilande
rich: abounding
with al the com-
moditie of the.
worlde.

D   saide

fayde that he fawe latin bookes in the Kings library, whiche they at this prefent doe not vnderftande, they haue a peculiar language and letters or caracters to them felues. They haue mines of all manner of mettals, but efpecially they abounde with golde. They haue their trade in Engroueland from whence they bring fkins and brimftone and pitch: And he faith that to y southwards, there is a great populous cõtrey very rich of gold. They sowe corne and make bere or ale, which is a kind of drinke that the north people doe vfe as we do wine. They haue mightie great woods, they make their buildings with wals, and there are many cities & caftels. They build fmal barkes and haue fayling, but they haue not the lodeftone nor know not the vfe of the cõpaffe. Wherfore thefe fifhers were had in great eftimatiõ, infomuch that the king fent them with 12. barkes to the fouthwardes to a countrey whiche they call Drogio: but in their voyage they had fuche countrary weather, that they thought all to haue perifhed in the fea, but yet efcaping that cruell death, they fel into another more cruel. For they were takẽ in the countrey and the moft parte of them eaten by the Sauage people, which feede vpon mans flefhe, as the fwecteft meate in their iudgementes that is.

But that fifher with his fellowes fhewyng them the maner of taking fifhe with nettes, faued their liues: and woulde goe euery day a fifhing to the fea and in frefh riuers, and take great aboundance of fifh and giue it to the chiefe men of the countrey, whereby hee got him felfe fo great fauour, that hee was very well beloued and honoured of euery one.

The fame of this man being fpred abroad in the countrey, there was a Lorde thereby that was verie defirous to haue him with him, and to fee howe hee vfed his miraculous arte of catching fifhe, in fo muche that he made warre with the other Lorde, with whom hee was before, and in the ende preuayling, for that hee was more mightie and a better warriour, the fifherman was fent vnto him with the reft of his company. And for the fpace of thirteene yeeres that hee dwelt in thofe partes, he faith, that he was fent in this order

to

Aboundance of golde.
trade from eftotiland, to Engroueland fkins, brimftone and pitche.
Gold, corne, and bere, or ale.
Many cities and caftles.

A countrey called Drogio.

The 6. fiſhermẽ of frifland only faued, by fhewing the maner to take fifhe.
The chiefeft of the 6. fifhers, fpecified before & his cõpanions

In the fpace of 13. yeres in Drogio.

to more than 25. Lordes, for they had continuall warre a-
mongest them selues, this Lorde with that Lord and he with
an other, onely to haue him to dwell with them, so that wan-
dring vp and downe the Countrey without any certayne a-
bode in one place, hee knewe almost all those partes. He saith
that it is a very great countrey and as it were a newe world,
the people very rude and voyde of all goodnesse, they goe all
naked so that they are miserablie vexed with colde, neyther
haue they the wit to couer their bodies w beastsskins, w they
take in huntinge, they haue no kind of metal, they liue by hunting, they carie certain lances of wood, made sharp at y point,
they haue bowes, the stringes whereof are made of beastes
skinnes : They are a very fierce people, they make cruell
warres one with another, and eate one an other, they haue
gouernours and certayne lawes verye diuers amongest
them selues. But the farther to the South westwardes, the
more ciuility there is, the ayre being somewhat temperat,
so that there they haue Cities, and temples to Idolls, wherein they sacrifice men and afterwardes eate them, they haue
there some knowledge and vse of gold and siluer.

Nowe this fisher hauing dwelt so many yeeres in those
countreys, purposed if it were possible to returne home into his countrey, but his companions dispayring euer to see it
agayne, let him goe in Gods name, they kept them selues,
where they were. Wherefore hee bidding them farewel,
fledde through the woods towardes Drogio, and was verie
well receiued of the Lorde that dwelt next to that place who
knewe him and was a great enemie of the other Lorde, and
so running from one Lorde to an other, being those by whom
hee had passed before, after long time and many trauelles
he came at length to Drogio where hee dwelt three yeeres.
When as by good fortune he heard by y inhabitants, y there
were certaine boates arriued vpon y coast, wherfore entring
into good hope to accomplish his intent, he went to y sea side &
asking the of what countrey they were, they answered of Estotiland whereat he was exceeding glad, and requested that

Sent to
more then
25. lords, which
continually war
red amongst the
selues for the
same fisherman.

3. yeres in Dro-
gio.

Where by happ
arriu. d certaine
boates from. E-
stotsland.

they

he became interpreter for y men that ariued at Dzozeo in the boates of Estotilande.

Afterwards hee frequ nted that trade with them in such sort, that he became very rich. And so furnished a bark of his owne & returned to Frislande where hee reported the story to his Lorde Zichmni.

Zichmni minded to send M. Antonio Zeno with a fleete towards those partes of Estotilande, and of 3. letter.

4. letter beginneth frō M. Antonio in Estotiland, to his brother Carlo in Venice.

The fisherman dead that should haue bin guid & interpreter.

Certaine marriners taken in his steede which came with him frō Estotiland.

July. Ile Ilofe.

they woulde take him into them, whiche they did verye willingly, and for that hee had the language of the Countrey and there was none of them coulde speake it they vsed him for their interpreter.

And after that hee frequented that trade with them, in such sorte that hee became verye riche and so furnishing out a barke of his owne hee returned into Frislande, where hee made reporte vnto this Lorde of that welthie Countrey.

And hee is throughly credited because of the Mariners, who approoue many straunge thinges, that hee reporteth to bee true. Wherefore this Lorde is resolued to sende me foorth with a fleete towardes those partes, and there are so manye that desire to goe in the voyage, for the noueltie and strangenesse of the thing, that I thinke we shall be very strongly appointed, without any publike expence at all. And this is the tenor of the letter before mentioned which I haue heere set downe, to giue intelligence of an other voyage, that M. Antonio made, being set out with many Barkes and men, notwithstanding hee was not captaine as hee had thought at the first hee shoulde, for Zichmni went in his owne person: & concerning this matter I haue a letter in forme as foloweth. Our great preparation for the voyag of Estotiland, was begun in an vnluckie houre, for three dayes before our departure, the fisherman died, that shoulde haue been our guid: notwithstanding this Lorde woulde not giue ouer the enterprize, but in steade of the fisherman tooke certayne Marriners that returned out of the Ilande with him, and so making our nauigation to the Westwards, we discouered certayne Ilandes subiect to Frislande, and hauing passed certayne shelues we stayed at Ledouo for the space of 7. dayes to refreshe our selues, and furnish the fleete with necessarie prouision. Departing from hence we arriued the first of July at the Ile of Ilofe, and for that the winde made for vs, wee stayed not there, but passed foorth, & being vpon the maine sea, there arose immediatly a cruell tempest wherewith for eight dayes space wee were miserably vexed, not knowing where wee were, and a great part of the Barkes were

were cast away, afterwarde waxing faire wether we gathe=
red vp the broken peeces of the Barkes that were lost, and
sayling with a prosperous winde wee discouered lande at
West.   Wherefore keeping our course directly vpon it, *Zichmni his first*
wee arriued in a very good and safe harborough, where wee *discouery of the*
sawe an infinite companie of people readie in armes, come *Iland Icaria.*
running very furiously to the water side, as it were for de=
fence of the Ilande .   Wherefore Zichimni causing his *Infinit numbei*
men to make signes of peace vnto them, they sent tenne men *of people in*
vnto vs that coulde speake tenne languages, but wee coulde *armes,*
vnderstande none of them, except one that was of Island. He *An Island man*
being brought before our Prince and asked, what was the *in Icaria.*
name of the Iland, and what people inhabited it,   and who
gouerned it, answered, that the Iland was called Icaria, and *Icaria Ilande.*
that all the kinges that had raigned there, were called Icari, *All the kings þ*
after the name of the first king of that place, which as they *had raigned in*
say was the sonne of Dedalus king of Scotland, who con= *that Ilad were*
quering that Iland, left his sonne there for king, and left the *called Icari af*
those lawes that they retaine to this present, and after this, he *ter the name of*
desiring to sayle further, in a great tempest that arose, was *þ place : which*
drowned, wherefore for a memoriall of his death, they call *they say was the*
those Seas yet, the Icarian Sea, and the kings of the Iland *sonne of Deda=*
Icari, and for that they were contented with that state, which *lus king of*
god had giue them, neither wholo they alter one iote of their *Scots.*
lawes and customes, they would not receiue any straunger, *Icarius drow=*
wherefore they requested our Prince, that hee woulde not *ned.*
seeke to violate their lawes, which they had receiued from *Icarian Sea.*
that king of worthie memorie and obserued very duly to that
present : which if hee did attempt, it woulde redounde to his
manifest destruction, they being all resolutely bent rather to
leaue their life, than to loose in any respect the vse of their
lawes.   Notwithstanding, that wee should not thinke they
did altogether refuse the conuersation and trafficke with
other men, they tolde vs for conclusion that they would wil= *The people of*
lingly receiue one of our men, and preferre him to be one *Icaria desirous*
of þ chiefe amongest them, only to learne my language the *of the Italian*
Italian tongue, and to bee enformed of our maners and cu= *tongue.*
                D 3   stomes,

stomes, as they had alreadie receiued those other tenne of
tenne sundzie nations, that came vnto their Jland. To these
things our Pzince answered nothing at all, but causing his
men to seeke some good harbozough, hee made signes as
though he would come on land, and sayling round about the
Jland, hee espied at length a harbozough on the East side of
the Jlande, where he put in with all his Fleet, the mariners
went on land to take in wood and water, which they did with
as great speede as they coulde, doubting least they shoulde
be assaulted by the inhabitants as it fell out in deed, foz those
that dwelt there abouts, making signes vnto the other with
fire and smoke, put them selues pzesently in armes and the
other comming to them, they came al running downe to the
Sea side vpon our men, with bowes and arrowes and other
weapons, that many were slaine and diuers soze wounded.
And we made signes of peace vnto them, but it was to no
purpose, foz their rage encreased moze and moze, as though
they had fought foz life and liuing.   Wherefoze wee were
fozced to depart and to sayle along in a great circuite about
the Jland, being alwaies accompanied vpon the hil tops and
the Sea coast with an infinite multitude of armed men, and
so doubling the Cape of the Jland towardes the Nozth, wee
found many great sholdes amongst the which foz the space of
ten daies we were in continual danger of loosing our whole
Fleete, but that it pleased God all that while to send vs very
faire weather. Wherefoze pzoceeding on till we came to ß
East cape, we sawe the inhabitaunts still on the hill tops &
by the Sea coast keepe with vs, and in making great outcries & shooting at vs a farre of they vttered their olde spite-
full affection towards vs.   Wherefoze we determined to
stay in some safe harbozough, and see if we might speak once
againe with the Islander, but our determination was fru-
strate, foz the people moze like vnto beastes than men, stood
continually in armes w intent to beat vs backe, if we shoulde
come on lande.   Wherefoze Zichmni seeing hee coulde
not pzeuaile and thought if hee shoulde haue perseuered and
followed

Hauing in that
Jland 10. men
of ten sundzy
nations.

Infinite multi-
tude of armed
men in Icaria.

followed obstinately his purpose, their victuals would haue failed them, hee departed with a faire winde and sailed sixe dayes to the Westwards, but the winde chaunging to the Southwest and the Sea waxing rough wee sayled 4. dayes with the wind in the powpe and at length discouering land, wee were afraide to approch neere vnto it, being the Sea growen, and we not knowing what lande it was, but God prouided for vs, that the winde ceasing there came a greate calme. Wherefore some of our companie rowing to land with oares, returned and brought vs word to our great comforte, that they had founde a very good Countrie and a better harborough, vpon which newes wee towed our ships & small Barkes to land, and being entred into the harborough, wee sawe a farre of a great mountaine, ÿ cast forth smoke, which gaue vs good hope that we shoulde finde some inhabitantes in ÿ Iland, neither would Zichmni rest, although it were a great way of, but send a 100. good souldiers to search the Countrie and bring report what people they were that inhabited it, and in the meane time they tooke in wood & water for the prouision of the Fleete, and catcht great store of fishe and Sea foule and founde such abundance of birdes egges that our men that were halfe famished, were filled withall. Whiles we were riding here, began the moneth of June, at which time the ayre in the Iland was so temperate and pleasant as is impossible to expresse, but when we coulde see no people at all, wee suspected greatly that this pleasant place was desolate and dishabited. Wee gaue name to the hauen calling it Trim, and the point that stretched out into ÿ sea wee called Capo di Trim. The 100. souldiers that were sent foorth, eight dayes after returned, and brought worde that they had been through the Ilande and at the mountaine and that the smoke was a naturall thing proceeding from a great fire that was in the bottome of the hill, and that there was a spring from which issued, a certaine matter like pitch, which ran into the Sea, and that there aboutes dwelt greate multitudes of people half wilde, hiding themselues in caues of

the.

the grounde, of small stature, and very fearefull, for as soone as they sawe them they fled into their holes, and that there was a great riuer and a very good harborough. Zichmni being thus enformed, and seeing that it had a holsome and pure ayre, and a very fruitefull soyle and fayre riuers with sundrie other commodities, fell into such liking of the place, that hee determined to inhabite it, and build there a Citie.
But his people being weary and faint with their long and tedious trauaile began to tumult and murmure, saying that they woulde returne into their Countrie, for that the winter was at hand, and if they entred into the harborough, they should not be able to come out againe before the next Sommer.

Wherefore hee retaining only the Barkes with Oares and such as were willing to stay with him, sent all the rest with the shippes backe againe, and willed that I, (though vnwilling) should bee their Captaine. I therefore departing, sayled for the space of twentie dayes to the Edwards without sight of any land, then turning my course towardes Southeast in fiue dayes I discouered lande and founde my selfe vpon the Ile of Neome and knowing the Countrie, I perceiued I was past Islande: wherefore taking in some fresh victuals of the inhabitants being subiect to Zichmni, I sayled with a faire winde in three dayes to Frisland, where the people, who thought they had lost their Prince, because of his long absence, in this our voyage, receiued vs very ioyfully.

Zichmni determining to remaine in the new discouered land, kept with him his barkes with oares, and men that were willing & sent the rest away homewards: Appointing Antonio Zeno chiefe captaine of them.
Antonio Zeno had sight of Neome, and knewe himselfe past Island.
Ende of the 4. letter.
A peece of a 5. letter.

What followed after this letter I know not but by coniecture, which I gather out of a peece of an other letter, which I will set downe heere vnderneath: That Zichmni builte a towne in the port of the Iland that hee discouered, and that hee searched the Countrie very diligently and discouered it all, and also the riuers on both sides of Engroueland, for that I see it particularly described in the Sea card, but the discourse or narration is lost. The beginning of the letter is thus. Concerning those things that you desire to knowe of mee, as of the men and their manners and customes, of the beastes and the Countries adioyning, I

Beginning of the letter.

haue

haue made thereof a particular booke, which by Gods helpe I will bring with mee: Wherein I haue described the countrie, the monstrous fishes, y customes and lawes of Frisland, Island, Estland, the kingdome of Norway, Estotiland, Drogio, and in the ende the life of master Nicolo, the knight our brother, with the discouerie which he made and of Groland. I haue also written the life and acts of Zichmni, a Prince as worthie of immortall memory, as any that euer liued, for his great valiancie and singuler humanitie, wherein I haue described the discouerie of Engroueland on both sides, and the Citie that hee builded. Therefore I will speake no further hereof in this letter, hoping to be with you very shortly, and to satisfie you in sundrie other thinges by worde of mouth. All these letters were written by master Antonio to master Carlo his brother. And it greeueth me, that the booke and diuers other writinges concerning these purposes, are miserably lost: For I beeing but a child, when they came to my handes, and not knowing what they were, (as the manner of children is) I tore them, and rent them in peeces, which now I cannot call to remembrance but to my greef. Notwithstanding, that the memory of so many good thinges shoulde not bee lost: whatsoeuer I could get of this matter, I haue disposed and put in order, in the former discourse, to the ende that this age might bee partly satisfied, to y which wee are more beholden for the great discoueries made in those partes, then to any other of the time past, beeing most studious of the relations of the discoueries of strange Countries, made by the great mindes, and industry of our auncetours.

This discourse was collected by *Ramusio* Secretarie to the state of Venice, (or by the Printer Tho. Giunti.)

Iohn Baptista Ramusio, died in *Padua* in Iuly, 1557.

¶ *The true and last discouerie of Flo-*
rida made by Captaine Iohn Ribault in the yeere
1562. Dedicated to a great noble man of Fraunce,
and translated into Englishe by one
Thomas Hackit,

Here as in the yeere of our Lorde God 1562. it pleased God to moue your honour, to choose and appoint vs, to dis-couer and view a certaine long coast of the West India, from the head of the lande called La-florida, drawing towarde the North part, vnto the head of Britons, distant from the saide

head of Laflorida 900. leagues, or there about : to the ends wee might certifie you & make true report of the tempera-ture, fertilitie, Portes, Hauens, Riuers, and generally of all the commodities that bee seene and found in that lande, and also to learne what people were there dwelling, which thing you haue long time agoe desired, beeing stirred therevnto by this zeale: That Fraunce might one day through newe discoueries haue knowledge of strange Countries, and also thereof to receiue (by meanes of continuall trafficke) riche and inestimable commodities, as other nations haue done by taking in hand such farre nauigations, both to the honor and prowes of their kings and princes, & also to the encrease of great profite and vse to their common wealthes, countries & dominions, which is most of all wout comparison to be conside-red & esteemed. It seemeth well y̆ yee haue been stirred here-vnto euen of God aboue, & led to it by the hope & desire you haue that a number of brutishe people and ignorant of Iesus Christe, may by his grace come to some knowledge of his holy Lawes and Ordinaunces . So therefore it see-meth that it hath pleased God by his godly prouidence to

reserue

referue the care which hee hath had of their faluation vntill this time, and will bring them to our faith, at the time by himfelfe alone forefeene and ordeined. For if it were needfull to fhewe howe many from time to time haue gone about to finde out this great lande, and to inhabite there : who neuertheleffe haue alwaies failed & beene put by from their intention and purpofe : fome by feare of fhipwrackes , and fome by great windes and tempeftes that droue them backe to their merueilous griefe. Of the which there was one

Sebaftian Gabota. a very famous ftranger named Sebaftian Gabota an excellent Pylot fent thither by king Henry, the peere 1498. and many others, who neuer could attaine to any habitation nor take poffeffion thereof one only foote of grounde, nor yet approche or enter into thefe parties and faire riuers into the which God hath brought vs. Wherefore (my Lorde) it may bee well faide that the liuing God hath referued this great lande for your poore feruantes and fubiectes, as well to the ende they might bee made great ouer this poore people, & rude nation : as alfo to approue the former affection which our kings haue had vnto this difcouerie.

For the late king Frances the firft (of happie memorie) a Prince endued with excellent vertues . The peere 1524. fent a famous and notable man a Florentine, named

John Verarza. Mafter John Verarzan, to fearch and difcouer the Weft parts as farre as might be : Who departing from Deepe with two veffels little differing from the making and burden of thefe two Pinnaces of the kinges, which your honour hath ordeined for this prefent nauigation. In the which land they haue found the eleuation the Pole, an viii. degrees. The Countrie (as he writeth) goodly, fruitfull, and fo good temperature, that it is not poffible to haue a better : beeing then as yet of no man feen, nor difcerned. But they being not able to bring to paffe at this firft voyage that which he had intended, nor to arriue in any Port, by reafon of fundrie incdueniences (which comoly happe) were coftrained to return into Fraunce : where after his arriuall, he neuer ceaffed to make
fuice

suite vntill he was sent thither againe, where at last he died.
The which occasion gaue small courage to sende thither a-
gayne , and was the cause that this laudable enterprise was
left of,vntill the yeere 1534.at which time his Maiestie,(desiring alwayes to enlarge his kingdome, countreys and dominions,and the aduauncing and ease of his subiectes) sent
thither a Pilote of S.Mallowes , a briton, named James
Cartier, well seene in the art and knowledge of Nauigati- James Cartier
on,& especially of the North parts,commonly called the new
land,led by some hope to find passage that waies to the south
seas : Who being not able at his first going to bring any
thing to passe,that he preteded to do: was sent thither againe
the yeere following, and likewise Le sire Hemerall, and as
it is well knowen they did inhabite and builde, and plant the
kings armies in the North part a good way in the lande, as
farre as Tauadu and Ochisaon . Wherefore(my Lord)
trust iustly that a thing so commendable and worthie to bee
with good courage attempted, that God woulde guid and
keepe vs,desiring alwayes to fulfill your commaundement.
When wee had done your businesse, and made our prepara-
tions the xviii.day of Februarie 1562 through the fauour of
God wee departed with our two vessels out of the hauen of
Claue de Grace into the road Caur:and the next day hoysted
vp saile(the winde being in y East)which lasted so fiue daies,
that we coulde not arriue at the nauch that is from betweene
the coast of Briton and Englande and the Iles of Surlinos
and Wiskam : So that the Winde blowing with great fu-
ry and tempest out of the West,and West Southwest, altogether contrary to our way and course,and all that we could
doe was to none effecte , besides the great daunger of breaking of our Mastes , as also to be hindered in our other labours. Wherefore as well to shonne many other inconueniences,which might follow to the preiudice and breach of our
voyage,hauing regard also to the likely daunger of death, y
some of our gentlemen and souldiers being troubled with
feuers and whot sicknesses,might haue fallen into : as also

foʒ other conſiderations, wee thought good to fall into the
road of Bʒeſt in Bʒitaine, to ſet there our ſick folke on land,
and ſuffer the tempeſt to paſſe. From whence (after wee
had taried there two dayes) wee returned againe to Sea-
warde to followe our nauigation, ſo that (my Loʒde) albeit
the winde was foʒ a long ſeaſon very much againſt vs, and
troubleſome: yet at the ende (God giuing vs thʒough his
grace and accuſtomed goodneſſe a meetely fauourable
winde) I determined with all diligence to pʒoue a newe
courſe which hath not beene yet attempted: trauerſing the
Seas of Oction 1800. Leagues at the leaſt, whiche in
deed is the true and ſhoʒt courſe that hereafter muſt be kept,
to the honour of our nation, reiecting the old conſerued opi-
on, which to long time hath beene holden as true.

Which is, as it was thought a thing impoſſible to haue
the winde at Eaſt, Noʒtheaſt, and keepe the race and courſe
wee enterpʒiſed, but that we ſhoulde be dʒiuen towarde the
region of Affrica, the Iles of Canaria, Madera, and other
landes there aboutes. And the cauſe why we haue beene the
moʒe pʒouoked and aſſured to take this new race, hath bin becauſe that it ſeemed to euery one, that we might not paſſe noʒ
goe in this Nauigation without the ſight and touching of
the Antillies and Lucaries, and there ſoiourne and take freſh
waters and other neceſſaries, as the Spaniards doe in their
voyage to new ſpaine: wherof (thanked be God) we haue had
no neede, noʒ entered the chanell of Roham: which hath bin
thought impoſſible. Foʒeſeeing alſo that it was not expedient
foʒ vs to paſſe thʒough the Ilandes, as wel to ſhune many inconueniences that might happen in paſſing that way (wherof
ſpʒingeth nothing but innumerable quarrels, pleadings, cō-
fuſions, and bʒeach of al woʒthy enterpʒiſes, and goodly nauigations, whereof enſueth complaintes and odious queſtions
betweene the ſubiectes of the king and his friends and alies)
as alſo to the ende they might vnderſtand, that in the time to
come (God hauing ſhewed vs ſuch graces, as theſe his wonderfull benefites firſte ſhewed to the pooʒe people of this ſo

goodly

goodly newe framing people, of so gentle a nature, and a countrey so pleasant and fruitefull, lacking nothing at all that may seeme necessarie for mans food)we would not haue to doe with their Ilandes,and other landes: which (for that they first discouered them) they keepe with much ielousie : trusting that if God will suffer the king (through your per-swation) to cause some part of this incomparable countrey to be peopled and inhabited with such a number of his poore subiectes as you shall thinke good, there neuer happened in the memory of man so great and good commoditie to France as this,and (my Lorde)for many causes, whereof a man is neuer able to say or write to the ful,as vnder the assured hope that we haue alwayes had in executing vprightly that which I had receiued in charge of you , God woulde blesse our wayes and nauigations. After we had constantly and with diligence in time conuenient determined vpon the way,wee shoulde haue thought it noysome and tedious to all our com-panie, if it had before bin knowen vnto any without tourning or wauering to or fro from their first ententio. And notwith-standing that satan did often what he could to sowe many ob-stractes,troubles and lettes, according to his acustomed sub-tilties,so it is come to passe, that God by his onely goodnes hath giuen vs grace,to make the furthest arte and trauars of the seas, that euer was made in our memorie or knowledge, in longitude from the East to the West:and therefore was it commonly sayde both in Fraunce and Spaine, and also a-mong vs,that it was impossible for vs safely to ariue thither, whither the Lord did conduct vs:Al which perswaded but of ignoraunce and lacke of attempting:which wee haue not bin afrayde to giue aduenture to prooue, Albeit that all Ma-riuers Cardes doe set the Coastes with shipwrackes with-out portes or Riuers : which wee haue found otherwise as it followeth.

Thursday the last of Aprill at the breake of the day , wee discouered and clearely perceyued a fayre Coast,stret-chyng of a great length couered with an infinite number of

high

high and fayre trees, wee being not past 7. or 8. leagues from
the shore, the countrey seeming vnto vs plaine without anye
shewe of hils, and approching neerer within foure or fiue leagues of the land, we cast an ancker at ten fadome water, the
bottome of the Sea being plaine with muche Ocias and fast
holde on the South side, as farre as a certaine point or Cape
situate vnder that Latitude of nine and twentie degrees and
a halfe, which we haue named Cape Francois.

Wee coulde espie neither Riuer nor Bay, wherefore
wee sent our Boates furnished with men of experience, to
sounde and knowe the coast neere the shore: who returning
to vs about one of the clock at after noone, declared that they
had founde among other thinges viii. fadome of water at the
harde bancke of the sea. Wherevpon hauing diligently
wayed vp our Anckers, and hoysted vp our sayles with wind
at will, we sayled and vewed the coast all along with vnspea-
ble pleasure, of the odorous smell and brauitie of the same.
And because there appeared vnto vs no signe of any Porte,
about the setting of the sunne we cast ancker againe: which
done, we did behold to and fro the goodly order of the woods
wherewith God hath decked euery way the sayd land. Then
perceiuing towarde the North a leaping and a breaking of
the water, as a streame falling out of the lande into the Sea.
For the whiche wee set vp sayles againe to double the same
while it was yet day. And as wee had so done, and passed be-
yond it: there appeared vnto vs a fayre entrie of a faire riuer
which caused vs to cast Ancker agayne there nerer the land:
to the end the next day we might see what it was, and though
that the winde blew for a time vehemently to the shoreward:
yet the hold and Anckerrage was so good, that one cable and
one Ancker helde vs fast, with out danger or sliding.

The next day in the morning, being the first of May,
wee assayed to enter this Porte, with two newe barges and
a boate well trimmed, finding little water barges whiche
might haue astonied and caused vs to returne backe to ship-
borde, if God had not speedily brought vs in. Where finding 3 6. fadome water, entred into a goodly and great riuer,
which

which as we went founde to encrease still in depth & large-
nesse,boyling and roaring through the multitude of all kind
of fish. This being entred wee perceiued a great number of
ÿ Indians inhabitants there,comming along the sandes &
Sea bankes,comming neare vnto vs, without any taking
of feare or doubt,shewing vnto vs the easiest landing place:
& thereupon we giuing them also on our parts thanks of assurance and friendlinesse. Forthwith one of appearance,out
of the best among them, brother vnto one of their kinges,or
gouernours,commaunded one of the Indians to enter into
the water : and to approch our boates to shew vs the coastes
landing place. We seeing this(without any more doubting
or difficultie)landed,and the messenger(after we had rewarded him with some looking glasse,and other pretie things of
small value)ran incontinently toward his Lord:Who forth
with sent mee his girdle, in token of assuraunce and friendship,which girdle was made of red leather, as well couered
and coloured as was possible:and as I began to go towards
him,hee set foorth and came and receiued me gently,and rei-
sed after his maner all his men,following with great silence
and modestie : yea more then our men did. And after we had
a while with gentle vsage congratulated with him : we fell
to the grounde a litle way from them,to call vpon the name
of God,and to beseech him to cōtinue still his goodnesse towards vs,and bring to the knowledge of our sauiour Christ
this poore people. While wee were thus praying (they sitting vpon the grounde,which was strawed and dressed with
Bay bowes)behelde and hearkened vnto vs, very attentiue-
ly without either speking or mouing: and as I made a signe
vnto their king,lifting vp mine arme,and stretching foorth
one finger,only to make them looke vp to heauen-ward:He
likewise lifting vp his arme towards heauen put foorth two
fingers:whereby it seemed that he made vs to vnderstande,
that they worshipped the Sunne and ÿ moone for Gods:as
afterwardes wee vnderstoode it so . In the meane time
their numbers increased, & thither came the kings brother,
that was first with vs,their mother, wiues, sisters and chil-

F
dren,

dzen, and being thus assembled, they caused a great number
of Bay boughes to bee cut, and therewith a place to be dzes=
sed foz vs, distant from theirs two fadom. Foz it is their ma=
ner to talke and bargaine sitting: and the chiefe of them to
bee apart, from the meaner sozt, with a shewe of great obe=
dience to their kinges, superiours, and elders. They bee all
naked, and of a goodly stature, mightie, & as well shapen &
propoztioned of body, as any people in y woild: very gentle,
curteous, and of a good nature.

The most part of them couer their raines and piuities
with faire Harts skinnes, painted most commonly with sun=
dzie colours: and the foze part of their body and armes, bee
painted with pzettie deuised woikes, of Azure, red, and
blacke, so well and so pzoperly as the best Painter of Eu=
rope coulde not amende it. The women haue their bo=
dies painted with a certaine Herbe like vnto Mosse, where=
of the Cedar trees, and all other trees bee alwayes couered.
The men foz pleasure doe alwayes trimme them selues
therwith, after sundzie fashions: They bee of tauny colour,
hauke nosed, and of a pleasant countenance. The women be
well fauoured, and will not suffer one dishonestly to appzoch
too neare them. But wee were not in their houses foz we
sawe none at that time.

After we had taried in this Nozth side of the riuer the
most part of the day (which riuer wee haue called May, foz
that wee discouered the same the firste day of the Moneth)
wee congratulated, made aliaunce, and entred into ami=
tie with them, and pzesented the king and his bzethzen with
Gownes of blewe cloth garnished with yellowe Flourede=
luces. And it seemed that they were soiy foz our departure:
so that the most part of them entred into the water vp to the
necke, to set our boates a flote.

Putting into vs sundzy kinde of fishes, which with mer=
ucilous speede they ranne to take in their packs, made in the
water with great Reedes, so well and cunningly set togea=
ther, after the fashion of a Laberinth, oz Maze, with so many
turnes

Why the riuer of May was so called.

turnes and crookes, as it is impoſſible to do it without much cunning and induſtrie.

But deſiring to imploy the reſt of the day on the other ſide of this riuer, to viewe and know thoſe Indians that wee ſawe there. We trauerſed thither, and without any difficultie landed amongeſt them, who receiued vs very gently and with great humanitie : putting vs of their fruites, euen into our boates, Mulberies, Raſpis, and ſuch other fruites as they founde ready by the way.

Soone after this came thither the king with his brethren, and others with bowes and arrowes in their handes, vſing therewithall a goodly and a graue faſhion, with their behauiour right ſouldierlike, and as warlike boldnes as may be. They were naked and painted as the other, their haire likewiſe long, and truſſed vp (with a lace made of herbes) to the top of their heads: but they had neither their wiues nor children in their companie. After we had a good while louingly enterteined and preſented them with like gifts of haberſher wares, cutting hookes and hatchets, and clothed the king & his brethren with like robes, as we had giuen to them on the other ſide: we entred and viewed the countrie thereaboutes, which is the faireſt, fruitfulleſt, & pleaſanteſt of al the world, abounding in hony, veniſon, wilde foule, foreſts, woods of all ſortes, Palme trees, Cypreſſe and Cedars, Bayes ẏ higheſt and greateſt, with alſo the fayreſt vines in all the world, with grapes accordding, which without natural art and without mans helpe or trimming will grow to toppes of Okes, and other trees that be of a wonderfull greatneſſe & height. And the ſight of the faire medowes is a pleaſure not able to be expreſſed with tongue : full of Hernes, Curlues, Bitters, Mallards, Egrepths, woodcocks, & all other kinde of ſmall birds : with Harts, Hindes, Buckes, wilde Swine , and all other kindes of wilde beaſtes, as we perceiued well both by their footing there, and alſo afterwardes in other places, by their crie and roaring in the night.

Alſo there be Conies & Hares: Silke wormes in merueilous number, a great deale fairer and better, then be our ſilk

wormes.

wormes. To bee ſhort, it is a thing vnſpeakeable to conſider the thinges that bee ſeene there, and ſhalbe founde more and more, in this incomperable lande, which neuer yet broken with plough yrons, bringeth forth al things according to his firſt nature, wherewith the eternall God indued it. About their houſes they labour and till the grounde, ſowing their fieldes with a graine called Mahis, whereof they make their meale: and in their Gardens they plant beanes, gourdes, cucumbers, Citrons, peaſon, and many other fruits and rootes vnknowen vnto vs . Their ſpades and mattockes be made of Wood, ſo well and fitly as is poſſible: which they make with certaine ſtones, oyſter ſhelles & muſcles, wherewith alſo they make their bowes and ſmal launces: and cut & poliſh all ſortes of wood, that they imploye about their buildings, and neceſſarie vſe: There groweth alſo many Walnut trees, Haſell trees, Cheritrees, very faire and great.

And generally wee haue ſeene, thereof the ſame ſimples and herbes that wee haue in Fraunce, and of the like goodneſſe, ſauour and taſte. The people be very good archers, and of great ſtrength: Their bowe ſtringes are made of Leather, and their arrowes of Reedes which they doe head with the teeth of fiſhes. As we now demaunded of them concerning ý land called Seuola, whereof ſome haue written not to bee farre from thence, and to bee ſituate within the lande, and toward the Sea called the South Sea. They ſhewed vs by ſignes that which we vnderſtood well enough, that they might goe thither with their Boates (by riuers) in twentie dayes. They that haue written of this kingdome and towne of Seuola, and other townes and kingdomes thereaboutes, ſay, that there is great aboundance of golde and ſiluer, precious ſtones, and other great riches: and that the people had their arrowes headed (in ſteede of yron) with ſharpe poi nted Turqueſſes. Thus the night approching, it was conuenient for vs to returne by day a ſhipboorde. Wee tooke leaue of them muche to their griefe, but more to ours without compariſon , for that wee
had

Seuola within xx. daies trauailing by boate of the riuer of May.

had no meane to enter the riuers with our shippe. And albeit, it was not their custome eyther to eate or drinke from the Sunne rising till his going downe : yet the king openly woulde needes drinke with vs, praying vs verie gently to giue him the cuppe whereout we had drunke: and so making him to vnderstande that wee woulde see him againe the next day, we retired to our shippes, which lay aboue sixe leagues from the hauen to the sea.

The next day in the morning we returned to land againe, accompanied with the Captaines, Gentlemen, and Souldiers, and other of our small trope : carieng with vs a Pillour or columne of harde stone, our kings armes graued therein, to plant and set the same in the enterie of the Porte in some high place, where it might bee easely seene, and being come thither before the Indians were assembled, we espied on the south syde of the Riuer a place very fitte for that purpose, vpon a litle hill, compassed with Cypres, Bayes, Paulmes and other trees, with sweete smelling and pleasant shrubbes. In the middle whereof we planted the first bound or limit of his Maiestie. This done, perceiuing our first Indians assembled, not without some misliking of those on the South parte, where we had set the limitte, who taried for vs in the same place where they met with vs the day before, seeming vnto vs that there is some enimitie betweene them and the others. But when they perceiued our long tarying on this side, they ran to see what we had done in that place where we landed first, and had set our limitte: which they vewed a great while without touching it any way, or abassing, or euer speaking to vs therof at any time after. Howebeit we could skāt departe but as it were w griefe of minde frō this our first alliance, they rowing vnto vs all along the riuer from all parts and presenting vs with some of their harts skins, painted and vnpainted, meale, litle cakes, freshe water, rootes like vnto Rinbabe which they haue in great estimation, and make therof a potion of medicine : also they brought litle bagges of redde colours and some small spices like vnto Gire, percey-

F 3 uing

uing among them selues fayre thinges painted as it had bin
with graine of scarlet, showing vnto vs by signes that they
had in the lande golde and siluer and copper : whereof wee
haue brought some. Also lead like vnto ours which we shewed. Also turquesses and great aboundance of pearles whiche
as they declared vnto vs they tooke out of oysters, whereof
there is taken euer along the riuer side, & among the reedes,
and in the marshes : and so merueylous aboundance as is
skant credible: and we haue perceiued that there be as many
and as faire pearles found there as in any countrey of the
worlde. For wee sawe a man of theirs as we entered into
our boates, that had a pearle hanging at a coller of golde and
siluer about his necke, as great as an Acorne at ỹ least. This
man as he had taken fishe in one of their fishing packs thereby brought that same to our boates, and our men perceiuing
the greatnesse therof, one of them putting his finger toward
it, the man drewe backe, and woulde no more come neare the
boate : not for any feare that he had that they woulde haue taken his Coller & Pearle from him for he would haue giuen
it them, for a looking glasse or a knife:

But that hee doubted lest they woulde haue pulled him into the boate, & so by force haue caried him away. He was one
of the goodliest men of all the company. But for that we had
no leasure to tary any longer with them, the day being well
passed, whiche greeued vs, for the commoditie and great riches, whiche as wee vnderstoode and sawe might bee gotten
there, desiring also to employ the rest of the day with our seconde aliance the Indians on the southside, as we perceiued
them the day before, which still taried looking for vs : Wee
passed the riuer to their shore, where as wee founde them tarying for vs, quietly and in good order, with newe paintings
vpon their face, and feathers vpon their heades: the King with
his Bowe and Arrowes lying by him, sate on the grounde
strawed with boughes betweene his two brethren, whiche
were goodly men and well shapen and of a wonderfull show
of actiuities, hauing vpon their heades, one haire trussed
vp-

Gold, siluer, and copper in Florida.
Turquesses and aboundance of pearles.
Marshes.

Pearles as big as acornes.

vpright of heyght, of some kinde of wild beast gathered and wrought together with great cunning, wrethed and fasted after the forme of a Diademe. One of them had hanging about his necke a rounde plate of redde copper well polished, with one other lesser of Siluer in the middest of it, & at his eare a litle plate of Copper wherewith they vse to stripe the sweat from their bodies. They shewed vs that there was great store of this mettell within the countrey, about fiue or sire dayes iourney from thence, both in the southside & northside of the same riuers, and that they went thither in their Boates. Which Boates they make but of one piece of a tree, woorking it whole so cunningly and featly, that they put in one of these boates fifteene or twentie persons, and go their wayes very safely. They that rowe stande vpright hauing their ores short after the fashion of a Peele. Thus being among them they presented vs with meale dressed & baked, very good & wel tasted, and of good nourishmēt, also beanes, and fish, as crabbes, lobstars, creuises, and many other kinde of good fishes, shewing vs by signes þ their dwellings were farre off, and if their prouision had been neere hande, they woulde haue presented vs with manye other refreshinges.

The night nowe approching, we were faine to returne to our Shippe, very much to our griefe: for that wee durste not hazarde to enter with our Shippe, by reason of a barre of sande, that was at the enterie of the Porte, howe be it, at a full Sea there is two fadome and a halfe of water at the least, and it is but a leape ouer a surge to passe this Barre, not passing the length of two cables, and then forthwith euery where within sire or seuen fadome water. So that it maketh a very fayre hauen, and Shippes of a meane burden from fourescore to a hundred tunnes may enter therein at all floodes, yea of a farre greater burthen, if there were French men dwelling there that might skoure the enterie as they doe in Fraunce: for there is nothing lacking for the lyfe of man. The situation is vnder the eleuation of xxx. degrees, a good climate healthfull, and of a good

F 4

temperature, merueilous pleaſãt, ỹ people good, & of a good
and amiable nature, which willingly will obay: yea be content to ſerue thoſe that ſhall with gentlenes and humanitie
goe about to allure them, as it is needful foʒ thoſe that be ſent
thither hereafter ſo to doe, and as I haue charged thoſe that
be left there to do, to the ende they may aſke and learne of thẽ
where they take their gold, copper, and turqueſſes, and other
thinges yet vnknowen vnto vs : by reaſon of the time we ſo-
iourned there. Foʒ if any rude oʒ rigoʒous meanes ſhould be
vſed towards this people, they woulde flie hither and thither
thʒough the Woods and Foʒeſts, and abandon their habita-
tions and countreys.

The next day being the thirde day of May, deſiring alwaies to finde out harbours to reſt in, we ſet vp ſaile againe:
And after we had raunged the coaſt as neere the ſhoʒe as we
could, there appeared vnto vs about ſeuen leagues of on this
ſide of ỹ riuer of May a great opening oʒ Bay of ſome riuer,
whither with one of our boates we rowed, & there found one
entrie almoſt like ỹ of the riuer of May, and within the ſame
as great a depth , and as large a diuiding it ſelfe into many
great ſtreames , great and bʒoade ſtretchinges towardes
the high lande , with many other leſſe, that diuide the countrey into faire and great landes and great number of ſmall
and fayʒe Medowes. Being entred into them about thʒee
leagues, wee found in a place very commodious, ſtrong, and
pleaſant of ſituation, certayne Indians, who receiued vs very gently: Howe be it, we being ſomewhat neare their houſes, it ſeemed it was ſomewhat againſt their good willes that
we went thither, foʒ at their cries and noyſes they made their
wiues and childʒen and hoſhoulde ſtuffe to be caried into the
Woods : Howe be it they ſuffered vs to goe into their houſes, but they themſelues woulde not accompany vs thither.
Their houſes bee made of Wood fitly and cloſe, ſet vpʒight
and couered with Reedes: the moſt part of them after the faſhion of a pauilion. But there was one houſe amongeſt the
reſt verie long and bʒoade, with ſettles rounde about made

of Reedes trimly couched together, which serue them both
for beddes and seates, they be of height two foote from the
grounde, set vpon great rounde pillers painted with red, yelowe, and blewe, well and trimlie polished: some sorte of this
people perceiuing that we had in no maner wise hurted their
dwellings nor gardens whiche they dressed very diligently,
they returned all vnto vs before our inbarking, seeming very
well contented by their giuing vnto vs water, fruites, and
Hart skinnes. It is a place wonderfull fertill, and of strong
situatiõ, the ground fat, so that it is likely that it would bring
forth Wheate and all other corne twise a yeere, and the com-   *Great fertilitie.*
modities for liuelihood, and the hope of more riches, bee like
vnto those we found and considered vpon the riuer of May,
without comming into the sea : this arme doth diuide, and
maketh many other Iles of May, as also many other great
Ilandes : by the which wee trauell from one Ilande to another, betweene lande and land. And it seemeth that men may   *Note.*
sayle without danger through al the countrey, and neuer enter into the great sea, which were a wonderfull aduantage.

This is the lande of Checere whereof some haue written,
& which many haue gone about to find out, for ŷ great riches
they perceiued by some Indians to be founde there. It is set
vnder so good a climate, that none of our men (though wee
were there in the hotest time of the yeere, the sunne entring
into Cancer) were troubled with any sicknesses. The people
there liue long and in great health and strength, so that the a-
ged men goe without staues, and are able to goe and runne
like the youngest of them, who onely are knowen to be olde
by the winckles in their face, and decay of sight. Wee departed from them veris friendly, & with their contentation.
But the night ouertaking vs, we were constrayned to lye in
our ships all that night, till it was day, floting vpon this riuer which we haue called Sene, because that the entery of   *The riuer of*
it is as broade as from hauer degrate vnto Honesleue. At   *Sene.*
the breake of the day wee espied out of the South syde one
of the fayrest, pleasauntest, and greatest nieedowe groundes
G   that

Heardes of tame Hartes.

that might bee seene, into the which wee went, finding at the very entrie a long, faire, and great Lake, and an innumerable number of footesteps of great Hartes and Hindes of a wonderfull greatnesse, the steppes beeing all fresh and new, and it seemeth that the people doe nourishe them like tame Cattell in great heards: for we saw the steppes of an Indian that folowed them.

The Chanell and depth of this riuer of Seyne, is one the side of the medowe that is in the Ile of May. Being returned to our ships, we sayled to knowe more and more of this coast, goyng as neere the shore as we coulde. And as wee had sayled about sixe or seuen leagues, there appeared vnto us another Bay, where we cast anker, and tarrying so all the night, in the morning wee went thither, and finding (by our sounding) at the entrie many bankes and beatings, we durst not enter there with our great ship, hauing named the riuer Somme, which is 8. 9. 10. 11. fadome depth, diuiding it selfe into many great Ilands, and small goodly medow grounds and pastures, and euery where such abundance of fish as is incredible, and on the Weast Northwest side, there is a great

Good hauens and riuers.

riuer that commeth fro the countrie of a great length ouer : and another on the Northeast side, which returne into the Sea. So that (my Lord) it is a countrie full of hauens, riuers, and Ilands, of such fruitfulnes as cannot with tongue be expressed : and where in short time great and precious commodities might bee found. And besides this wee discouered

7. Great & good riuers.

and found also vii. riuers more, as great and as good, cutting and diuiding the land into faire and great Ilands. The Indians inhabitants there be like in manners, & the countrie in fertillitie apt and commodious through out to beare & bring foorth plentifully all that men would plant or sowe vpon it. There bee euery where the highest and greatest Firtrees that can be seene, very well smelling, and where out might bee gathered (with cutting the only bark) as much Rosen, Turpentine, & Frankesence, as men would desire. And to be short there lacketh nothing. Wherefore being not able to enter & lie with our great vessels there, we could make no long abiding,

ding,nor enter so farre into the riuers and countries as wee would faine haue done: for it is well knowne how many inconueniences haue happened vnto men,not only in attempting of newe discoueries, but also in all places by leauing their great vessels in the Sea,farre from the land, vnfurnished of the heads and best men. As for ye other riuers we haue giuen them names as followeth: and vnto the Ilandes ioyning vnto them,the same name that the next riuer vnto it hath),as you shall see by the portratures or Cardes ye I haue made thereof. As to the fourth name of Loire, to ye fift Charnet,to ye sirt Carõ to the 7.riuer Belle,to ye 8.riuer Graũde, to the 9.port Royall,and to the tenth Belle Airrir. *Maps and Sea Cardes.*

Upon Whitsunday the xxvii.day of May,after wee had perceiued and considered that there was no remedie, but to assay to find the meanes to harber our ships,as wel to amend and trimme them,as to get vs fresh water,wood, and other necessaries,whereof wee hauing opinion that there was no fayrer or fitter place for the purpose, then port Royall.And when wee had sounded the entrie and the Chanell (thanked be God) wee entered safely therein with our shippes, against the opinion of many , finding the same one of the fayrest and greatest Hauens of the worlde. *Port royall a most excellent hauen.*

Howe be it , it must be remembred least men approching neare it within seuen leagues of the lande,bee abashed and afraide on the Eastside,drawing towarde the Southeast, the grounde to be flatte,for neuerthelesse at a full sea, there is euery where foure fadome water,keeping the right Chanel. *Note.*

In this part there are many riuers of meane bignesse and large , where without daunger the greatest shippes of the worlde might bee harboured, which wee founde, no Indian inhabiting there aboutes. The Porte and Riuers side is neerer then tenne or twelue leages vpwardes into the countreys,although it bee one of the goodliest, best, and fruitefullest countreys that euer was seene , and where nothing lacketh , and also where as good and likely commodities bee founde as in other places thereby.

For wee founde there a great number of Pepertrees, *Pepper trees.* the

the Pepper yet greene, and not ready to bee gathered: Also the best water of the world, and so many sortes of fishes that yee may take them without net or angle so many as ye will. Also an innumerable sort of wilde foule of all sortes, and in little Ilandes at the entrie of this hauen, on the East North-east side, there is so great number of Egrepes that the bushes bee all white and couered with them, so that one may take of the young ones with his hande as many as hee will carry away. There bee also a number of other foules, as Hernes, Bitters, Curlues, And to bee short, there is so many small byrdes that it is a strange thing to bee seene. Wee founde the Indians there more doubtfull and fearefull then the others before: Yet after we had been in their houses, and congregated with them, and shewed curtesie to those that we founde to haue abandoned there through boats meale, victuall, and small housholde stuffe, and both in not taking awaye or touching any part thereof, and in leauing in that place where they dressed their meate, Kniues, Looking glasses, little Beades of glasse, which they loue and esteeme aboue golde and pearles, for to hang them at their eares and neck, and to giue them to their wiues and children: they were somewhat emboldened.

A speciall note.

For some of them came to our boates, of the which wee carried two goodly and strong aboorde our shippes, clothing and vsing them as gently as it was possible. But they ceased not day nor nyght to lament, and at length they escaped away. Wherefore albeit, I was willing (according to your commaundement and memoriall) to bring away some of them with vs, on the Princes behalfe and yours, I forbare to doe so for many considerations and reasons that they told mee, and for that we were in doubt that (leauing some of our men there to inhabite) all the Countrie, men, women, and children, woulde not haue ceased to pursue them for to haue theirs againe: seeing they bee not able to consider and way to what entent wee shoulde haue carried them away: & this may bee better doone to their contentation, when they haue better acquaintance of vs, and know that there is no suche crueltie

A commande-ment.

crueltie in vs, as in other people and nations, of whom they haue beene beguiled vnder colour of good faith: whiche doing in the ende turned to the doers no good. This is the riuer of Iordain in mine opinion, whereof so much hath beene spoke, which is very faire & the coūtrie good, both for ye easie habitation, and also for many other things, which should bee long to write. *The riuer of Iordan.*

The twentie of May wee planted another columne or pillor grauen with the kinges armes on the South side, in a high place, of the entrie of a great riuer, which wee called Libourne: where there is a lake of fresh water very good, and on the same side a little lower towards the entrie of the Hauen is one of the fayrest fountaines that a man may drink of, which falleth by violence down to the riuer from an high place out of a red and sandy ground, and yet for all that fruitefull and of good ayre, where it shoulde seeme that the Indians haue had some faire habitation.

There we sawe the fayrest & the greatest vines with grapes according, and young trees, and smal woods, very wel smelling, that euer were seen: wherby it appeareth to be the pleasantest & most commodious dwelling of al ye world. Wherefore (my Lorde) trusting you will not thinke it amisse (considering the commodities that may be brought thence) if we leaue a number of men there, which may fortifie and prouide them selues of things necessary: for in all new discoueries it is the chiefest thing that may be done, at the beginning to fortifie and people the countrey. I had not so soone set forth this to our companie, but many of them affraid to tary there, yet with such a good will and ioly corage, that such a number did thus offer themselues, as we had much to do to stay their importunitie. *Exceeding faire and great vines* *Fortification most necessarie in all newe discoueries.*

And namely of our shipmaisters and principall pilotes, and such as we could not spare. How bee it, wee lefte there but to the number of thirtie in all, Gentlemen, souldiers, and marriners, and that at their own suit and prayer, and of their owne free willes, and by the aduice and deliberation of the Gentlemen sent on the behalfe of the Prince and yours. *30. lefte behind at their owne suite*

And

And haue left vnto the forehead and rulers (following therein your good will) Captaine Albert de la Pierria, a fouldier of long experience, and the firft that from the beginning did offer to tarry. And further by their aduice, choyfe and will, infkaled and fortified them in an Iland on the north fide, a place of ftrong fituation and commomodious, vpon a riuer which wee named Chenonceau, and the habitation and Fortreffe Charlefote.

They fortified in an Iland.

After we had inftructed and duly admonifhed them of that they fhoulde doe (as well for their maner of proceeding, as for the good and louing behauiour of them) the xi. day of the moneth of Iune laft paft, we departed from port Royal: minding yet to range and view the coaft vntill the xl. degrees of the eleuation: But for as much as there came vpon vs troublefome and cloudie weather, very incommodious for our purpofe, and confidering alfo amongft many other thinges, that we had fpent our cables and furniture thereof, which is the moft principall thing that longeth to them that go to difcouer countreys, where continually both night and day they muft lie at ancker: alfo our victualls beeing perifhed and fpilte, our lacke of Boatefwaines to fet forth our rowe barges, and leaue our veffels furnifhed. The declaration made vnto vs of our Pilots and fome others that had before been at fome of thofe places, where we purpofed to fayle, and haue been already found by fome of the kings fubiects, the daunger alfo and inconueniences that might thereof happen vnto vs: & by reafon of the great myftes and fogges wherof the feafon was already come, we perceiued very well wheras we were, y we could do no good, & that it was to late, & y good & fit feafon for to vndertake this thing already paft. Al thefe thinges thus well confidered and wayed, and alfo for that we thought it meet and neceffarie that your honour fhould with diligence be aduertifed (through the help of God) to returne homewards to make relatiõ vnto you of the effect of our nauigation. Praying God that it may pleafe him to keepe you in long health, and profperitie.

Fortie degrees of eleuation.

Miftes & fogs when they come.

FINIS.

Notes in writing besides more

ptiuie by mouth that were giuen by a Gentleman,
Anno, 1 5 8 0. to *M. Arthure Pette* and to *M. Charles Iack-*
man, sent by the marchants of the Muscouie companie for the
discouerie of the northeast strayte, not altogether vnfit
for some other enterprises of discouerie, hereafter to bee taken in hande.

What respect of Ilandes is to be had, and why.

Hereas the Portingales haue in their
course to their Indies in the Southeast,
certaine portes and fortificatiõs to thrust
into by the way, to diuers great purposes: So you are to see what Ilands, and
what portes you had neede to haue by the
way in your course, to the Northeast. For which cause I
wish you to enter into consideration of the matter, & to note
all the Ilands, & to set them downe in plat, to two endes, that
is to say, That wee may deuise to take the benefite by them.
And also foresee how by the the Sauages or ciuill Princes,
may in any sort annoy vs in our purposed trade that way.

And for that the people to the which wee purpose in this
voyage to goe, be no Christians, it were good that the masse
of our commodities were alwayes in our owne disposition,
and not at the will of others. Therefore it were good that
we did seeke out some small Iland in the Scithian Sea,
where we might plant, fortifie, & Staple safely, frõ whẽce
(as time shoulde serue) wee might feede those heathen
nations with our commodities without cloying them, or
without venturing our hole masse in the bowels of their
countrey.

And to whiche Iland if neede were (and if we shoulde
thinke so good) we might allure the Northeast nauie, the nauie of Cambalu to resort with their commodities to vs there
planted, and stapling there.

P   And

And if such an Jland might be found so standing as might
shorten our course, and so standing, as that the Nauie of Cābalu, or other those parties might cōueniently saile vnto th-
out their dislike in respect of distāce: thē would it fal out wel.
For so, besides lesse daūger, and more safetie, our ships might
there vnlade and lade againe, and returne the selfesame sommer to the ports of England or of Norway.

And if such an Jland may be found for the stabling of our
commodities, to the which they of Cambalu would not saile,
yet we might, hauing shippes there, imploy them in passing
betweene Cambalu and that stapling place.

Respect of hauens and harbarowes.

ANd if no such Jlandes may be found in the Scithiā sea
toward the firme of Asia, then are you to search out the
ports that be about Noua Sembla all along the tract of that
land, to the end you may winter there the first yeere, if you be
let by contrarie winds, & to the ende that if wee may in short
time come vnto Cābalu, & vnlade and set saile againe for returne without venteriug, there at Cābalu, that you may on
your way come as farre in returne as a port about Noua Sē-
bla: That the Sommer following, you may the sooner be in
England for the more speedy vent of your East cōmodities,
and for the speedier discharge of your Mariners: if you can
not goe forward and backe in one selfe same sommer.

And touching the tract of the land of Noua sembla , toward the East out of the circle Artick in the more temperate
zone, you are to haue regard, for if you finde the soyle planted with people, it is like ꝥ in time an ample vēt of our warm
wollē clothes may be founde. And if there be no people at al
there to be found, then you shall specially note what plentie
of whales, & of other fish is to be found there, to the end wee
may turne our newfoūd land fishing or Island fishing, or our
whalefishing, ꝥ way for the ayde & cōfort of our new trades
to the Northeast, to the coasts of Asia.

Respect of fishe and certayne other thinges.

And

AND if the ayre may be found vpon that tract temperate, & the soyle yeelding wood, water, land and grasse, and the seas fish, then we may plant on that mayne the offals of our people, as the Portingals doe in Brasil, & so they may in our fishing in our passage, & diuers wayes yeelde commoditie to England by harbouring and vitelling of vs.

And it may bee, that the inland there may yeelde mastes, pitch, tarre, hempe, and all thinges for the Nauie, as plentifully as Eastland doth.

The Ilandes to be noted with their commodities and wantes.

TO note the Ilands, whether they be hie lande or lowe land, moũtanie, or flat, sandy, grauelly, clay, chalchy, or of what soyle, woodđy or not woodđy, with springs & riuers or not, and what wyld beasts they haue in the same.

And whether there seeme to be in the same apt matter to build withall, as stone free or rough, and stone to make lime withall, and wood or coale to burne the same withall.

To note the goodnes or the badnes of the hauens, & harborowes in the Ilandes.

If a straite be founde what is to bee done and what greate importance it may bee of.

AND if there be a strayte in the passage into the Scithian Seas, the same is specially and with great regard to bee noted, especially if the same straite be narrow and to be kept, I say it is to be noted as a thing that doeth much importe, for what Prince soeuer shall be Lorde of the same, and shall possesse the same, as the king of Denmarke doth possesse the straite of Denmarke, he onely shall haue the trade out of these regions into the Northeast partes of the world for himselfe, and for his priuate profit, or for his subiectes only, or to enioy wonderfull benefite of the toll of the same, like as the king of Dẽmarke doth enioy of his straites, by suffering the Merchantes of other Princes to passe that way, If any such straite be found, the eleuation, the hie or lowe lande, the ha-

uens neere, the length of the straites, & all other such circū-
staunces are to be set downe for many purposes : And all the
Mariners in ÿ voyage are to be sworne to keepe close al such
thinges, that other Princes preuent vs not of the same, after
our returne vpon the disclosing of the mariners, if any suche
thing should happe.

Which way the Sauage may be made able to purchase our cloth and other their wantes.

IF you finde any Iland or mayne lande populous, and that
the same people hath neede of cloth : Then are you to deuise what commodities they haue to purchase the same
withall.

If they be poore, then are you to consider of the soyle, and
how by any possibilitie the same may be made to enrich thē,
that hereafter they may haue somthing to purchase the cloth
withall.

If you enter into any mayne by portable riuer, and shall
finde any great woods, you are to note what kynd of timber
they be of : That we may know whether they are for pitche,
tarre, mastes, deleborde, clapborde, or for buylding of ships or
houses, for so if the people haue no vse of them they maye be
brought perhaps to vse.

Not to venture the losse of any one man.

YOu must haue great care to preserue your people, since
your number is so small , and not to venture any one
man in any wise.

To bring home besides marchandize certaine trifles.

BRing home with you (if you may) from Cambalu, or o-
ther ciuill place, one or other young man, although you
leaue one for him.
Also the fruites of the countries, if they will not of thēselues
dure, drie them, and so preserue them.

And bring with you the Curnelles of peres, & apples, and
the stones of such stone fruites as you shall finde there.

A

Also the seedes of all strange herbes and flowres, for such seedes of fruites and hearbes comming from another part of the world and so farre off, wil delite the fancie of many, for the strangenes and for that the same may growe and continue the delite long time.

If you arriue at Cambalu or Quinsay, to bring thence the Mappe of that Countrey, for so shall you haue the perfecte description which is to great purpose.

To bring thence some old printed booke, to see whether they haue had print there, before it was deuised in Europe as some write.

To note their force by sea and by lande.

If you arriue in Cambalu or Quinsay, to take a speciall viewe of their Nauie, and to note the force, greatnesse, maner of building of them, the sayles, the tackels, the anckers, the furniture of them, with ordinaunce, armour, and munition.

Also, to note the force of the walles and bulwarkes of their cities, their ordinaunce, and whether they haue any caliuers, and what powder and shot.

To note what armour they haue.

What swordes.

What pikes, halbertes and billes.

What horses of force, and what light horses they haue.

And so throughout, to note the force of the countrey, both by sea and by lande.

Things to be marked to make coniectures by.

TO take speciall note of their buildings, and of the ornaments of their houses within.

Take a speciall note of their apparell and furniture, & of the substance that the same is made of, of which a marchant may make a gesse, as well of their commodities as also of their wantes.

To note their shoppes and warehouses and with what

commo=

commodities they abounde, the price also.

To see their shambles, and to viewe all such thinges as are brought into the markets, for so you shall sone see the commodities, and the maner of the people of the inlande, and so giue a gesse of many things.

To note their fieldes of grayne, and their trees of fruite, and howe they abounde or not abounde in one and other, and what plentie or scarcetie of fishe they haue.

Thinges to be carried with you, whereof more or lesse is to be caried for a shewe of our commodities to bee made.

KErsies of all orient coulours, specially of stamel, brodecloth of orient colours also.

Frisadoes, motleys, bristowe frices, spanish blankettes, bayes of all collours, specially with stanell, wolseds, carels, sayes, wedmoles, flanelles, rashe, &c.

Feltes of diuers colours.

Taffeta hats.

Deepe cappes for mariners coloured in stamell, whereof if ample vent may be found, it woulde turne to an infinite commoditie of the common poore people by knitting.

Quilted Cappes of leuant Taffeta of diuers colours, for the night.

Knit stockes of silke of orient colours.

Knit stockes of Jersey yerne, of orient colours, whereof if ample vent might followe the poore multitude shoulde be set in worke.

Stocks of kersey of diuers colours for men and for women.

Garters of Silke of seuerall kindes, and of colours diuers.

Girdels of Buffe, and all other leather, with gilt and vngilt Buckles, specially wast girdels, wast girdles of veluet.

Gloues of all sortes, knit and of leather.

Gloues perfumed.

Points

Poyntes of all sortes of silke, threed, and lether, of all manner of colours.

Shooes of spanishe leather, of diuers colours, of diuers lengthes, cut and vncut.

Shooes of other leather.

Veluet shooes, and pantoples.

These shooes and pantoples to be sent this time, rather for a showe then for any other cause.

Purses knit, and of leather.

Night cappes knit and other.

A Garnishe of Pewter, for a showe of a vent of that englishe commoditie, Bottelles, flagons, spoones, &c. of that metall.

Glasses of englishe making.

Venice glasses.

Looking glasses for women, great and fayre.

Small dials a few for proofe, although there they wil not hold the order they do heere.

Spectacles of the commom sort.

Others of Cristall trymmed with siluer and otherwise.

Owre glasses.

Commes of Iuorie.

Commes of Boxe.

Commes of Horne.

Linen of diuers sorts.

Handkerchewes with silke of seuerall colours wrought.

Glasen eyes to ride with against dust.

Kniues in sheathes, both single and double, of good edge.

Needles great and small of euery kinde.

Buttons greater and smaller, with mouldes of leather and not of wood, and such as be durable of double silke, and that of sundrie colours.

Boxes with weightes of golde, and of euery kinde of the coyne of golde, good and badde, to shewe that the people here, vse weight and measure whiche is a certayne showe of wisedome, and of a certayne gouernment setled here.

All the seuerall siluer Coynes of our Englishe moneys, to bee caried with you to bee showed to the gouernours at Cambalu, which is a thing that shal in silence speake to wise men more then you imagine.

Lockes and keyes, hinges, boltes, haspes, &c. great and small of excellent worke in a shippe, whereof if vent may bee hereafter, wee shall set our subiectes in worke, whiche you must haue in great regarde. For in finding ample vente of any thing that is to be wrought in this realme, is more worth to our people besides the gaine of the marchant, then Christchurch, Bridewel, the Sauoy, and all the Hospitals of Englande.

For banketing on Shipborde, persons of credite.

First the sweetest perfumes to set vnder hatches to make the place sweete against their comming aborde, if you arriue at Cambalu, Quinsey, or in such great cities and not among sauages.

Marmelade.

Sucket.

Figges barelled.

Reysings of the sunne.

Comfets of diuers kindes made of purpose, that shall not dissolue by him that is most excellent.

Prunes damaske.

Dried peres.

Walnuttes.

Almondes.

Smalnuttes.

Oliues to make them taste their wine.

The Apple Iohn that dureth two yeeres to make showe of our fruites.

Hullocke.

Sacke.

Vials of good sweet waters, & casting bottels of glasses to besprinckel the gests withall, after their comming aborde.

Suger, to vse with their wine, if they will.   The

The sweete oyle of Sancie and excellent French vineger, and a fine kinde of Bisket, stiped in the same doe make a banketting dishe, and a little Suger cast in it cooleth and comforteth, and refresheth the spirites of man.

Synomome water ⎫ is to be had with you to make a shew
Imperiall water ⎬ of by taste, and also to comfort your
⎭ sicke in the voyage.

With these and such like, you may banket where you arrive the greater and best persons.

Or with the gift of these Marmelades in small boxes, or small violles of sweete waters you may gratifie by way of gift, or you may make a merchandise of them.

The mappe of England and of London.

Take with you the mappe of Englande set out in faire colours, one of the biggest sort I meane, to make shewe of your Countrie from whence you come.

And also the large mappe of London, to make shewe of your Citie. And let the riuer bee drawne full of shippes of all sortes, to make the more shewe of your greate trade and trafficke in trade of merchandise.

Ortelius booke of mappes

If you take Ortelius booke of mappes with you, to marke all these regions, it were not amisse, and if neede were to present the same to the great Cam, for it would bee to a Prince of merueilous account.

The booke of the attyre of all nations.

Such a booke carried with you and bestowed in gift, woulde be much esteemed, as I persuade my selfe.

Bookes.

If any man will lende you the newe Herball, and suche bookes as make shewe of Herbes, Plantes, Trees, Fishes, Foules and Beastes of these regions, it may much delight

the

the great Cam, and the nobilitie, and also their merchants to haue the viewe of them: for all things in these parties so much differing from the thinges of those regions, since they may not be here to see thē, by meane of the distance, yet to see those things in a shadowe, by this meane will delight them.

The booke of Rates.

Take with you the booke of Rates, to the ende you may pricke all those commodities there specified that you shall chaunce to find in Cambalu, in Quinsey, or in any part of the East, where you shall chaunce to bee.

Parchment.

Rowles of Parchment, for that we may vent much with-out hurt to the Realme, and it lyes in small roome.

Glewe.

To carrye Glewe, for that wee haue plentie, and want vent.

Red Oker for Painters.

To seeke vent because wee haue great mines of it, and haue no vent.

Sope of both kindes.

To trie what vent it may haue, for that we make of both kindes, and may perhaps make more.

Saffron.

To trie what vent you may haue of Saffron, because this Realme yeeldes the best of the worlde, and for the tillage and other labours, may set the poore greatly in work to their reliefe.

Aquauitæ.

By newe deuise wonderfull quantities may bee made heere, and therefore to seeke the vent.

Blacke Conie skinnes.

To trie the vent at Cambalue, for that it lyes towardes
the

the North, and for that wee abounde with the commoditie, and may spare it.

Threade of all colours.

The vent thereof may set our people in worke.

Copper Spurres, and haukes belles.

To see the vent, for it may set our people in worke.

A note and a caueat for the merchant.

That before you offer your commodities to sale that you indeuour to learne what commodities the Countrie there hath.   For if you bring thither veluet, taffeta, spice, or any such commoditie that you your selfe desire to lade your selfe home with, you must not sell yours deare, least hereafter you purchase theirs not so cheape as you woulde.

Seedes for sale.

Carrie with you for that purpose, all sortes of Garden seedes, as well of sweete strawing herbes and of flowers, as also of pot herbes, and all sorts for rootes, &c.

Leadde of the first melting.

Leadde of the second melting of the slagges.

To make triall of the vent of Leadde of all kindes.

English yron, and wyer of yron and copper.

To trye the sale of the same.

Brymstone.

To trie the vent of the same, because wee abounde of it made in the Realme.

Anthimoney a minerall.

To see whether they haue any ample use there for it, for that wee may lade whole nauies of it, and haue no vse of it vnlesse it bee for some small portion in founding of belles, or a lithel that the Alcumistes vse, of this you may haue two sortes at the Appoticaries,

Timber

Tinder boxes with Steele, flint, and matches, and
tinder, the matches to bee made of Gineper, to
auoide the offence of brimstone.

To trie and to make the better sale of Brimstone by shewing the vse.
Candles of waxe to light.

A painted Bellowes.

For that perhaps they haue not the vse of them.
A pot of cast yron.
To trie the sale, for that it is a naturall commoditie of
this Realme.
All maner of edge tooles.
To bee sold there or to the lesse ciuill people by the way
where you shall twich.

What I woulde haue you there to remember.

To note specially what excellent dying they vse in these
regions, and therefore to note their garments, & ornaments
of houses : and to see their die houses and the materialles,
and simples that they vse about the same: and to bring Mu-
sters and shewes of the colours and of the materials, for that
it may serue this clothing realme to great purpose.

To take with you for your owne vse.
All maner of Engyns to take fishe and foule.

To take with you those thinges that bee in
perfection of goodnesse.

For as the goodnesse nowe at the first may make your
commodities in credit in time to come : So false and so-
phisticate commodities shall drawe you and all your commodities into contempt and ill opinion.

❧ Notes framed by a Gentleman

heretofore to bee giuen to one that pre-
pared for a difcouerie, and went not: And not
vnfitt to be committed to print, confidering the fame
may ftirre vp confiderations of thefe and of fuch
other thinges, not vnmeete in fuch new
voyages as may be attempted
hereafter.

That the firft Seate be chofen
on ý feafide fo as (if it may be)
you may haue your owne Nauie within Bay, riuer oz lake,
within your feat fafe from the
enemie. And fo as the enemie
fhalbe foꝛced to lie in opē rode
abꝛoade without, to be difper-
fed with all windes and tempefts that fhall arife. Thus
feated you fhall bee leaft fubiecte to annoy of the enemie, fo
may you by your Nauie within, paffe out to all partes of the
woꝛlde, and fo may the fhippes of Englande haue acceffe to
you to fupply all wantes, fo may your commodities be caried away alfo. This feate is to bee chofen in temperate Cli-
mat, in fweete ayꝛe, where you may poffeffe alwayes fweete
water, wood, feacoles, oꝛ turfe, with fifh, flefh, grayne, fruits,
herbes and rootes, oꝛ fo many of thofe, as may fuffice very
neceffitie foꝛ the life of fuch as fhall plant there. And foꝛ the
poffeffing of mines of golde, of filuer, copper, quickfiluer, oꝛ
of any fuche pꝛecious thing, the wantes of diuers of thofe
needfull thinges may be fupplied from fome other place by
fea, &c.

Stone to make Lyme of.   ⎧ are to be looked foꝛ as
  Slate ftone to tile withall ⎪ thinges without which
oꝛ fuche clay as maketh tyle, ⎪ no Citie may bee made
  Stone to wall withal if ⎩   R   noꝛ

Brycke may not bee made,
Timber for building easely to be conueied to the place,
Reede to couer houses or such like, if tile or slate be not.
nor people in ciuill sorte be kept together.

The people there to plant and to continue are eyther to liue without trafficke, or by trafficke and by trade of marchandize. If they shall liue without sea trafficke, at the first they become naked by want of linen and wollen, and very miserable by infinite wantes that will otherwise ensue, and so will they be forced of them selues to depart, or els easely they will bee consumed by the Sp. by the Fr. or by the naturall inhabithantes of the countrey, and so the interprice becomes reprochfull to our nation, and a lett to many other good purposes that may be taken in hande.

And by trade of marchandize they can not liue, excepte the sea or the lande there may yeelde commoditie for commoditie. And therefore you ought to haue most speciall regarde of that point, and so to plant, that the naturall commodities of the place and seate, may drawe to you accesse of Nauigation for the same, or that by your owne Nauigation you may carie the same out, and fetche home the supplye of the wantes of the seate.

Such nauigation so to bee employed, shall besides the supply of wantes, bee able to encounter with forreyne force.

And for that in the ample vente of suche thinges as are brought to you out of engl. by sea, standeth a matter of great consequence, it behoueth that all humanitie and curtesie and much forbearing of reuenge to the inland people be vsed, so shall you haue firme amitie with your neyghbours, so shall you haue their inland commodities to maintayne trafficke, & so shall you waxe rich and strong in force. Diuers & seuerall commodities of the inland are not in great plentie to be brought to your handes, without the ayde of some portable or Nauigable ryuer, or ample lacke, and therefore to haue

the

the helpe of suche a one is most requisite : And so is it of
effecte for the dispersing of your owne commodities in exchange into the inlandes.

Nothing is more to be indeuoured with the Inland people then familiaritie. For so may you best discouer al the naturall commodities of their countrey , and also all their
wantes,all their strengthes,all their weakenesse, and with
whome they are in warre, and with whome considerate in
peace and amitie,&c. whiche knowen , you may woorke
many great effectes of greatest consequence.

And in your planting the consideration of the climate and
of the soyle bee matters that are to bee respected . For if
it be so that you may let in the salt sea water,not mixed with
the fresh into flattes , where the sunne is of the heate that it
is at Rochell,in the Bay of portingall,or in Spaine , then
may you procure a man of skill, and so you haue wonne
one noble commoditie for the fishing , and for trade of marchandize by making of Salt.

Or if the soyle and clymate bee such as may yeelde you
the Grape as good as that at Burdeus, as that in Portingale, or as that about Siui in Spaine,or that in the Ilands
of the Canaries,then there resteth but a woorkeman to put
in execution to make wines, and to dresse Resings of the
sunne and other,&c.

Or if you finde a soyle of the temperature of the South
part of Spaine or Barbarie, in whiche you finde the Olif
tree to growe: Then you may bee assured of a noble marchandize for this realme , considering that our great trade
of clothing doth require oyle, and weping howe deere of
late it is become by the vent they haue of that commoditie in
the West Indies,and if you finde the wilde olif there it may
be graffed.

Or if you can finde the berrie of Cochenile with whiche
wee colour Stammelles , or any Roote, Berrie ,Fruite,
wood or earth fitte for dying ,you winne a notable thing fitt

for our state of clothing. This Cochenile is naturall in the west Indies on that firme.

Or if you haue hides of beastes fit for sole Lether,&c. It wilbe a marchandize right good,and the sauages there yet can not tanne Lether after our kinde, yet excellently after their owne maner.

Or if the soyle shall yeeld or Figges, Almondes, Sugar Canes,Quinces, Orenges , Lemons, Potatos, &c. there may arise some trade and trafficke,by figges,almonds, sugar,marmelade,Sucket &c.

Or if great woods bee founde,if they be of Cypres,chests may bee made,if they bee of some kinde of trees, pitche and tarre may be made, if they bee of some other then they may yeelde Rosin,Turpentine,&c.and al for trade and trafficke, and Caskes for wine and oyle may be made: likewise ships and houses,&c.

And because trafficke is a thing so materiall,I wish that great obseruation be taken what euery soyle yeeldeth naturally,in what commoditie soeuer, and what it may be made to yeeld by indeuour,and to send vs notice home,that thereuppon wee may deuise what meanes may be thought of to rayse trades.

Nowe admit that we might not be suffered by the sauages to enioy any whole countrey or any more then the scope of a Citie, yet if wee might enioy trafficke and be assured of the same, wee might bee much inriched, our Naue might be increased,& a place of safetie might there be found,if change of religion or ciuill warres shoulde happen in this realme, which are thinges of great benefite. But if we may inioy any large Territorie of apt soyle,we might so vse the matter,as we should not depende vpon Spaine for oyles,sacks, resinges,orenges,lemons,Spanish skinnes,&c. Nor vppon Fraunce for woad,baysalt,and gascoyne wines, nor on Estlande for flaxe,pitch,tarre,mastes,&c. So we shoulde not so exhaust our treasure, and so exceedingly inriche our doubtfull friendes,as we doe,but shoulde purchasse the commodities that we want for halfe the treasure that now we do: but
should

ſhould by our own induſtries & the benefits of the ſoile there
cheapely purches oyles,wines, ſalt,fruits,pitch,tarre,flaxe,
hempe,maſtes,boordes, fiſhe,gold, ſiluer, copper, tallowe,
hides and many commodities: beſides if there be no flatts to
make ſalt on, if you haue plentie of wood you may make it
in ſufficient quantitie for common vſes at home there.

If you can keepe a ſafe hauen, although you haue not the
friendſhip of the neere neyghbours, yet you may haue trafficke by ſea vpon one ſhore or other,vpon that firme in time
to come,if not preſent.

If you finde great plenty of tymber on the ſhore ſide or
vpon any portable riuer,you were beſt to cut downe of the
ſame the firſt wynter,to bee ſeaſoned for ſhippes, barkes,
botes and houſes.

And if neere ſuch wood there be any riuer or brooke vpon
the which a ſawing mill may be placed, it woulde doe great
ſeruice,and therefore conſideration woulde bee had of ſuche
place.

And if ſuch port & choſe place of ſetling were in poſſeſſiõ &
after fortified by art,although by ŷ land ſide our Engliſhmẽ
were kept in,and might not inioy any traffick with the next
neighbours,nor any vittel:yet might they vittel themſelues
of fiſh: to ſerue verie neceſſitie, and enter into amitie with
the enemies of their next neighbours,& ſo haue vent of their
marchandize of England and alſo haue vittel,or by meanes
herevpon to be vſed to force the next neighbours to amitie.
And keeping a nauie at the ſetling place,they ſhoulde finde
out along the tracte of the lande to haue trafficke , and
at diuers Ilandes alſo. And ſo this firſt ſeate might in
time become a ſtapling place of the commodities of many
countreys and territories, and in tyme this place myght become of all the prouinces round about the only gouernour.
And if the place firſt choſe ſhould not ſo wel pleaſe our people,as ſome other more lately founde out: There might bee
an eaſie remoue, and that might be raſed, or rather kept for
others of our nation to auoyde an ill neyghbour, &c.

If the ſoyles adioyning to ſuch conuenient hauen and
ſetling

ſetling places be founde marſhie and boggie, then men ſkil-
ful in draining are to be caried thither. For arte may worke
wonderfull effectes therein, and make the ſoyle rich for many vſes.

To plante vppon an Ilande in the mouth of ſome notable riuer, or vpon the poynt of the lande entring into the riuer, if no ſuch Iland be, were to great ende. For if ſuch riuer
were nauigable or portable farre into the lande, then would
ariſe great hope of planting in fertill ſoyles, and trafficke on
the one or on thother ſide of the riuer, or on both, or the lin-
king in amitie with one or other petie king contēding there
for dominion.

Such riuers founde, both barges and boates may bee
made for the ſafe paſſage of ſuch as ſhal perce ẏ ſame. Theſe
to bee couered with doubles of courſe linnen artificially
wrought, to defend the arrow or the dart of the ſauage from
the rower.

Since euery ſoyle of the world by arte may be made to
peelde things to feede and to cloth man, bring in your returne a perfect note of the ſoyle without and within, and we
ſhall deuiſe if neede require to amende the ſame, & to draw it
to more perfectiō. And if you finde not fruits in your planting place to your liking, we ſhal in v. drifats furniſh you tẘ
ſuch kinds of plants to be caried thither ẏ winter after your
planting, as ſhall the very next ſummer folowing, yeeld you
ſome fruite, and the yere next folowing, as much as ſhal ſuf-
fice a towne as big as Callice, and that ſhortly after ſhall be
able t o yeeld you great ſtore of ſtrong durable good ſider to
drinke, & theſe trees ſhalbe able to increaſe you within leſſe
then vii. yeres as many trees preſently to beare, as may ſuf-
fice the people of diuers pariſhes, which at the firſt ſetling
may ſtand you in great ſteade, if the ſoyle haue not the commoditie of fruites of goodneſſe already. And becauſe you
ought greedily to hunt after thinges that peelde preſent reliefe, without trouble of cariage thither, therefore I make
mencion of theſe, thus ſpecially, to the ende you may haue it
ſpecially in mynde.

FINIS.   The

The names of certaine commodities growing in part of *America, not presently* inhabited by any Christians frō Florida Northward, *gathered out of the discourses, of Verarzanus, Thorne, Cartier, Ribalt, Theuet, and best, which haue bin personally in those Countreys, and haue seene these things amongst many others.*

Beastes.

Leopardes.
Stagges.
Hartes.
Deare.
Beares.
Hares.
Wildeswine.
Connyes.
White beares.
A beast farre bigger then an oxe.
Wolues.
Dogges.
A kinde of beast like a Conny.
Beuers.
Marterns.
Foxes.
Bagers.
Otters.
Weesels.
A beast called Su being like a Bull.

Birdes.

Haukes.
Bitters.
Curlewes.
Herons.
Woodcockes.
Partridges.
Small birdes.
Plentie of foule for al pleasant game.
Aporates.
Blackbirdes.
Cranes.
Crowes like Cornish Choughes.
Duckes.
Godettes.
Geese.
Pigions.
Margaues,

Feasants.
Swannes.
Thrushes.
Turtles.
Finches.
Nightingales. &c.

Fishes.

Coddes.
Salmons.
Seales.
Makerels.
Tortoyses.
Whales.
Horsefishes.
A fish like a grayhound good meate.
Lampreys.
Crabbes.
Crefishes.
Lobsters.
Eeles.
The riuers full of incredible store of all good fishe.

Wormes.

Silke wormes fayre and great.

Trees.

Bay.
Cypres.
Damson.
Palme.
Many trees yeelding sweet sauour.
Okes.
Nut trees.
Firre.
Uines.
Cahene good against poyson.
Cedars. Hasell trees.
Cheritrees. Walnuttrees.
Pepper trees.
Ameda which healeth many diseases.

Asshe.
Boxe.
Citron.
Yewe.

Elmes.
Whitelmes.
Pynes.
Willowes.

Filbirdtrees better then ours.
Whitethornes bearing a berrie as big
   as a Damson.
Vines bearing a great grape.

Fruites.

Cowcumbers.
Cytrons.
Raspis.
Apples.
Damsons.

Gourdes.
Mulberries.
Almonds.

Reasons great and small.

Melons.
Figges.

Muske melons.
Orenges.
Strawberries.

Lemons.
Dates very great.

Gooseberries red and white.

Gummes.

Rosen.
Turpentine.
Frankencense.

Pitche.Tarre.
Honnie.
Ware.

Spices and Drugges.

Pepper.
Small spices like to vire.
Reubarbe in Florida : diuerse other
   kindes.

Hearbes and floures.

Many sortes of herbes differing from
   ours.
Many simples like those of Fraunce.
Hempe.
Parsley.

Roses.

Redde.
White.
Damaske.

Grayne and Pulse.

Corne like Rie.
Dates.
Peason.

Myllet.
Beanes of diuers
coulers.

Another strange corne of good nourish-
   ment.
Maiz.

Metalles.

Golde in good quantitie.
Siluer.
Coper.
Leade.
many like other Mineral matter.

Precious stones.

Turqueses.
Rubies.
Pearles great and faire.
Precious stones of diuers colours.
Turqui a stone much esteemed there.
Riph a kind of stone shining bright.

Other stones.

Marble very hard.
Alabaster.
Quarries of glistring stones.

Jasper.
Freestone.

Colours.

Yelowe.
Blewe.

Redde.
Scarlet.
Roane colour.

Deareskinnes wrought like branched
   Damaske.
Harts skinnes paynted and died of di-
   uers colours.
Bagges of red colours.
A roote called Auaty that they dye red
   withall in Florida.

So as the commodities already knowen,
   besides many yet vnknowen are
      these, and that in great
         quantitie.

Flesshe.
Fishe.

Fruites.
Grayne.

Beueradges or drink of diuers sortes.
Golde.
Siluer.

Copper.
Lead.

Pearles.
Spices.
Drugges.

Furres.
Feathers.
Gummes.
Oyles.

Silke.
Hides vndressed.
Beasts skins wrought like Damaske.
Lether died.
Hartes skinnes painted.
Stones for fayre building.
Precious stones.
Colours.
All kinde of good wood.

Imprinted at London at the
three Cranes in the Vine-
tree, by Thomas Daw-
son. 1582.